DATE DUE

DEMCO 38-296

The book rings true to the urgency of history in the making. Dr. Scott deftly shows us the changing face of the Great Sleeping Giant and its emergence from a long hibernation.

Ken Kelley
Journalist, *San Francisco Focus*

Gini Scott has done it! She has conveyed what I and many other citizen diplomats know in our souls: the joys, and trials, the confusion, the sadness, the love of meeting and befriending ordinary Soviet citizens. The Open Door *will allow readers a taste of what it is like to 'get off the tour' and know those who for so many years have been called our 'enemy.' This delightful work will inspire many to go and find out for themselves, and they will do so much better prepared for having read it. But even if you don't leave home, this book will take you inside, behind the propaganda images, to the heart of Soviet society, a journey that will open your heart.*

Philip W. Bennett
Co-Director of Citizens
Network for Common
Security

The Open Door *is an engaging experience of the Soviet people at the genesis of the opening up of the U.S.S.R. It demonstrates a new approach to travel—that of 'citizen diplomacy'—which strengthens the bonds of peace and understanding between people.*

Jacqueline Mathes
Research Director
Beyond War

It is must reading for a person who wants a picture of what is happening in the Soviet Union since glasnost *and* perestroika *have come into existence.*

> Howard Frazier
> Executive Director
> Promoting Enduring Peace

If it is impossible to take your own trip to the Soviet Union, The Open Door *will take you there in a very personal and relaxed way. A good travelogue, far better than most, because of the personalized experience.*

> Proctor Jones
> Author of *Classic Russian Idylls*
> and *At the Dawn of Glasnost*

. . . very interesting and useful for anyone who wants to go to the Soviet Union.

> Alex Harris
> President, General Tours

A very pleasant, easy-reading journal of a trip through the Soviet Union as a citizen diplomat. Ms. Scott is very sensitive to the warm feelings that develop in such a situation and communicates them very well.

> Willis Harman
> President
> Institute of Noetic Sciences

THE OPEN DOOR

THE OPEN DOOR
Traveling in the U.S.S.R.

Gini Graham Scott

New World Library
San Rafael, California

© 1990 Gini Graham Scott
Published by New World Library
58 Paul Drive
San Rafael, CA 94903

Cover design: Thom Dower
Text design and illustrations:
Nancy Benedict
Photographs: Gini Graham Scott
Typography: Walker Graphics

First printing, May 1990

ISBN 0-931432-62-6

Printed in the U.S.A. on acid-free paper

Today we stand poised at the beginnings of a new world order because of the changes transforming the Soviet Union and spreading out to Eastern Europe, Western Europe, and the world. This book is dedicated to this spirit of change, to the journey we all are now taking into the future, and to the Soviet people and the leaders who are helping to move us into this bold new world that even now is being created and recreated.

Two years ago I had the chance to witness the first hesitant openings of the door to this transformation, when I traveled to the Soviet Union as part of a citizen diplomacy trip.

That summer of 1988 was a time of exploration and experimentation, the time of the historic Party Congress that began the process of transforming the political system. On our trip we were continually made aware of how things had already begun to change a little in the past few years; now suddenly there was even more hope and expectation of further changes to come. We were there at a very special moment, standing in that doorway of history between the old and the new, seeing the new created and nurtured by the old.

For me, *The Open Door* describes this moment of history, as we experienced it on our trip. I feel privileged that I was there to see and record this, because it helps to provide a basepoint for understanding the current happenings, like a marker, a guidepost at the beginning of a long journey that helps to chronicle the journey by showing the point at which it begins.

Contents

Acknowledgments

I want to thank the many people who contributed in some way to the creation of this book.

First and foremost, my thanks to the many wonderful Soviet people we met on our trip, who gave of their time and hospitality and shared their thoughts and their hearts with us.

Secondly, my thanks to our trip leader, Barbara O'Reilly, who helped us in meeting with many of these people and helped to make our trip an enjoyable adventure with her warmth and enthusiasm. She also was of assistance in reviewing the manuscript. In addition, special thanks to some of the people on the trip who contributed their comments and suggestions, especially Jane Burnett, as well as Eleanor Mitchell and Rebecca Dawson. Thanks, too, to the Center which sponsored my trip.

Additionally, I want to thank my editor, Cheryl White, who did a heroic job in editing the manuscript down to size, and then editing again to reflect the tremendous changes that have occurred and are occurring even now in the Soviet Union. And finally, thanks to my publisher, Carol LaRusso, and the rest of the staff at New World Library, who had the faith to believe in this book and the role of the individual traveler in helping to create bonds of friendship to further Soviet-American relations.

Introduction

In the last few years a unique approach to travel has grown in popularity, particularly between the United States and the Soviet Union. Called "citizen diplomacy," it differs from the typical travel experience in its emphasis on personal contact between people from different countries. Its goal is to have people meet and come to understand each other better—individually and collectively—sharing their lives, their experiences, their hopes and dreams.

While "citizen diplomats" enjoy many of the usual tourist attractions such as sightseeing, shopping, and night life, they also spend time with the local people, participating in their daily activities and conversations, visiting their homes, accompanying them to local events. When we step inside another culture, not only our curiosity, but our heart is engaged. And in a world growing more aware each day of the need for global cooperation, it can be an exciting way to explore the many avenues of peaceful exchange.

This type of travel to the Soviet Union has been expanding rapidly partly because of the growing numbers of Soviet-American friendship and dialogue groups, over 2,000 of them flourishing in America today. In addition, the spirit of *glasnost* (openness to disclose and debate shortcomings) has created a groundswell of interest in the Soviet Union. In 1989 alone, over 150,000

Americans visited the U.S.S.R., the largest number ever; even more are expected in 1990.

Citizen diplomats have a more global purpose than ordinary tourists in that they serve as representatives of their country, working to promote peace, friendship and understanding. They are changemakers. Even one person has the ability to make a difference. Imagine this multiplied many thousands of times over! As the awareness and consciousness of ordinary people change, their influence becomes considerable—sufficient to help change government attitudes and shift international policies. This well-known quote by Dwight D. Eisenhower chronicles the global changes now happening: "One day people are going to want peace badly enough that governments are going to have to get out of their way and let them have it."

The Open Door describes my own experience as a citizen diplomat and suggests how others might use this approach for their own travel. I was inspired to go on this kind of trip because of the legal studies tour of the Soviet Union I took in the summer of 1987. We met with Soviet officials from various legal institutions, including the Soviet Bar Association, and sat in on a Soviet trial. While these meetings did provide a glimpse of everyday Soviet life, laws, and institutions, I felt a desire to know more, to get closer to the Soviet people we were meeting. Certainly our hosts were extremely polite, generous, and entertaining—I will long remember the sumptuous spread of fruit, wine, and Soviet delicacies laid out for us and the warm welcoming speech and toasts made on our behalf by the lawyers and judges from the court we attended in Baku, the capital of Azerbaijan. Yet I wanted to further penetrate this more "public" veneer. I came away with dozens of questions and a ripe curiosity about the Soviet people. What were the more personal stories behind *glasnost* and *perestroika* (restructuring)?

During this initial trip I conceived the idea for a board game to further Soviet-American understanding, called *Glasnost: The Game of Soviet-American Peace and Diplomacy.* In the process of producing my new game, I came in contact with a center that sponsors citizen diplomacy trips to the Soviet Union. While attending an educational presentation there in February of 1988, I discovered that the group had several such trips planned, and that one designed for professionals in all fields was leaving in June—right in the middle of my summer vacation from law school. I decided to go.

This book is one of the results of my trip. It is an account of what happened to me and other members of my group as we traveled about, met Soviet people, and exchanged perceptions, feelings, and attitudes about our lives and the historic changes taking place, and which continue to take place even more rapidly now. I have changed the names and identities of both the Soviets we encountered and the people in my group in order to protect their privacy.

Numerous facts and statistics on the U.S.S.R. are included—much of it provided by the Center which sponsored our trip and by our Soviet tour guides. I made every effort to record information accurately and to check and update material, but since things are changing so quickly in the U.S.S.R., the resources listed at the end of the book should be consulted to help provide the most current available information.

In the final chapter there is some information on how to prepare for a citizen diplomacy trip, whatever the destination. The Appendix lists some organizations sponsoring trips to the Soviet Union and other countries. Going with an organized group, as I did, is a lot of fun and helps to provide good contacts, background information, and personal support, although you may simply want to use the organizations as a resource if you decide you would rather travel on your own.

But whether you are planning to go to the Soviet Union or are reading *The Open Door* as an armchair traveler, I hope my trip will come alive for you, and that you will be inspired to share this book and its ideas with your friends. Today is an exciting time for us all because we live in a time of such historic change, undreamed of just a few short years ago, and the transformations in the Soviet Union now are literally remaking the world order. In this time of change there is much tumult and confusion, and now, more than ever, the U.S.S.R. and all the countries of our small interconnected world need friends, business partners, and ambassadors of peace. We each can participate in our own way. I hope this book contributes to our world effort and will help to bring about a changed, more enlightened, peaceful world.

Now, I invite you to go through the open door and join me in my adventures as a citizen diplomat in the U.S.S.R.

Gini Graham Scott

PART I

GETTING THERE

CHAPTER 1

Getting There—
Getting Acquainted

The uncertainties we experienced with our itinerary during the three months before our departure seemed to echo the changes taking place in the Soviet Union itself in that eventful summer of 1988. For a while it even looked as if we might not go. As it happened, our trip dates coincided with the opening of the historic Party Congress at the Kremlin, so we would have to be bumped out of Moscow during this time due to accommodations shortages. As a result, we could not get the all-important Intourist confirmation number, which all travelers to the U.S.S.R. must have, until an alternate itinerary could be worked out, if at all.

Our tour leaders, a bubbly, energetic woman named Betty and her husband, Kurt, rose to this challenge and spent long hours working to smooth out the arrangements and ensure our departure. Betty, always optimistic, reassured us at regular intervals, so we tried to relax and devote this time to learning about life in the Soviet Union and the citizen diplomacy approach we would be using. We would then have some foundation on which to set our new experience, be able to ask more intelligent, sensitive questions, and have a deeper understanding of the people we were about to meet. The object was to get past the usual Soviet stereotypes, don the glasses of a different culture, and adjust our vision accordingly.

3

To this end we studied Soviet history, education, and economics; we absorbed information about Gorbachev and his
regenerative reforms; we gained overviews in such areas as
government, the roles of women, and religious attitudes; and we
practiced our Russian! The need for our brief lesson on the
Russian language was obvious. If we were going to get around
on our own and meet the people, we had to at least be able to
read the signs, which would be written in Cyrillic, and we had
to know how to pronounce what we read. We also needed to
know some of the basics in order to make everyday requests
such as "I want some coffee," or "Where is the metro station?"
or "Where is the hotel?" and to this end the Center sent us lists
of common words, phrases, and questions, and pronunciation
tapes.

The pre-trip learning was a fascinating journey in itself.
For example, I had believed that the terms "Russian" and
"Soviet" were synonymous, but this isn't so. Even though Russian is the official language of the Soviet Union, the Soviet
population consists of over 100 nationalities who live in 15
separate and autonomous republics—each with its own language and sometimes with its own alphabet. Although the Russian Republic, which includes Moscow, Leningrad, and Siberia
as well, is the largest of the Soviet republics, spanning eleven
time zones, Russians now account for only fifty-two percent of
the entire population. In addition, the birthrate of other groups
is currently much higher.

The Center had sent us handouts on everything we would
need to know in order to become effective citizen diplomats,
grooming us for exploration into areas where we might learn
from each other or join to find solutions in our age of rapid and
perpetual change. Hopefully, our small expedition would add to
the cumulative effect of changing global attitudes, more freedom and prosperity for all, and, ultimately, peace.

About three weeks before we were supposed to leave, a
meeting was called at Betty and Kurt's house. Though we still
didn't have our confirmation number, Intourist had at least

replied to our travel agent with an offer of a shorter itinerary with different cities. We could still go to Moscow and Leningrad, but instead of Tbilisi and Kiev, we would go to Vilnius (in Lithuania) and Minsk (in Belorussia) and spend the extra time relaxing in Helsinki, Finland, or other parts of Scandinavia.

It was a crazy kind of take-it-or-leave-it situation, but we didn't have much choice. Then Betty came up with an alternative possibility, which turned out to be one of the highlights of the trip. Perhaps Nadya, her contact in Kiev who was part of a youth organization there, could work out transportation and hotel arrangements for us. We could then keep Kiev in the proposed itinerary and travel outside the usual Intourist cloak of protection for just that period of time. It was an arrangement normally unheard of in the Soviet Union at the time and might be difficult to arrange in that, to quote Betty, "there are only twenty-five phone lines from the U.S. to Moscow, and they all go out of Philadelphia." But at least she could try.

Only a few days before we were scheduled to leave, Betty called to say it had all come together. Somehow Nadya had been able to arrange for transportation to Kiev and convince Intourist that she could properly take care of us during our stay there. "It seems miraculous," Betty said. "I think we have done the impossible."

We were elated by the time we reached the San Francisco airport. The trip we had all been preparing for and anticipating so long was finally about to begin! I wheeled on my carry-on luggage, which included a heavy camera case, portable typewriter, my *Glasnost* game and buttons, flyers, and about a half-ream of paper, so I could capture just about everything that happened on the trip.

And ironically, one of the most memorable experiences happened in Seattle, where we stopped to change planes and pick up a few more people for our group. Betty had asked us to check our luggage to Seattle, not direct to Helsinki, so we could personally pick it up and take it to our Helsinki flight. "That way," Betty explained, "we can connect with our luggage and make sure it really gets on the flight."

So we had our first experience of looking for luggage tagged with red ribbons as it came out of the chute. Forming a bedraggled procession, we dragged, pushed, and wheeled our large suitcases and often our bulky hand luggage with their bright red bows to a terminal about two buildings away. I felt we were on a chain gang, as Betty cheered us on. "Just a little further, just a little further," she chanted.

And then, as we waited, heaving and panting in line, waiting to recheck our bags, about a dozen men in their twenties and thirties who were wearing blue and white satin jackets with the letters "U.S.A." on the back strode up. They were part of a professional hockey team that was traveling to the U.S.S.R., and one of them, a big brawny man with a mustache, pointed to a large wooden bat wrapped up in a white foam rubber pad, which Mike and Rowenna were carrying with their children's luggage.

"Hey, are they letting you take that on?" the man pointed and pouted.

"Yeah," piped one of the others, a smaller thinner man with a wiry frame. "We wanted to take our hockey sticks on with our hand luggage. But they wouldn't let us do it. They said the Soviets might think these were weapons. Now can you imagine that? So we had to pack them away."

"But," said a third, who rippled with muscles, "at least they didn't say anything about the fireworks which we're taking in."

"Fireworks?" Mike repeated, and at that a half-dozen of us at the end of our line turned around to listen closely.

"Sure, fireworks," said the man with muscles. "We're going to be in Moscow on July 4th, and we're going to set them off in Red Square." He grinned. "And drink some beer."

"Yeah, we'll really light up the sky," smiled the big man with the mustache. "What better way to celebrate Independence Day than with fireworks in Red Square."

"But fireworks? Isn't that illegal?" asked Rowenna.

"And couldn't it be dangerous?" queried Angela.

But the man with the mustache just shrugged his shoulders. "Aw, heck, what's the big deal. We'll just tell them we're Americans."

"Yeah," added the man with the muscles. "It'll be a great celebration. A great thing to remember. We'll really show them something they've never seen. Independence Day in the Square."

Several of the men in the group laughed, as if they expected to be pulling off a great joke on the Russians by having this celebration there. It was as if they saw this as a way to show off American values and thumb their noses at what they considered opposing Russian beliefs.

Of course, the men didn't say all this. But as a group, those of us who heard them speak felt this was the underlying message they were expressing, and we cringed. Here we were going to try to promote understanding, and be open to looking at things from the Soviet view; in contrast, here was this group of fellow Americans, traveling to the Soviet Union at exactly the same time, representing almost a complete opposite. It was like confronting the image of the "ugly American" we were trying to overcome. We whispered among ourselves, as if to diminish this threat.

"But how can they do this?" asked Rowenna.

"They'll surely try to stop them," said Mike.

"They'll probably be arrested," stated Jennifer.

"And I hope they are," said Angela. "They think they can go into another culture and do whatever they please, show off and make a mockery of what the Soviets think and believe. What nerve. It almost makes me ashamed to say I'm an American, too. And they wear jackets that say U.S.A., as if they speak for all Americans. Well, they don't speak for me." She glared at the group of hockey players and turned away in a huff.

And then the rest of us turned away, hoping that by looking away we could shut them out. For they represented exactly the image of the unempathetic, brash, and brassy American that we wanted to erase.

This very brief encounter lasting for just minutes struck a

deep chord with our group, and for a long time, waiting in line, people continued to mutter about it. Later, in discussions and at meetings, the thought of the hockey group would come up again.

But at least, when we got on the plane, we didn't have to interact with them again for we were, perhaps quite appropriately, at opposite ends of the plane—we toward the front in the no-smoking section, all of them far in the back. And later we saw them only once again when we got off the plane and claimed our luggage in Finland. Then we went our separate ways, though their memory lingered on.

When we arrived in Helsinki, stiff from our long plane ride, we began what would become a regular ritual: counting our luggage and pushing our way through crowds to look for our tour guide. We soon spotted her, a short pert woman who ushered us to a waiting bus, cheered us in our travel weariness with some highlights about Helsinki, and led us into the large hotel with marble columns where we would be staying. In what would be the usual practice each time we arrived at a hotel, we turned in our passports to Betty and received the keys to our rooms.

A few hours later, after resting and freshening up, we had our first group meeting. Until now, most of the other people on the trip were still a blur to me—just names, faces, and snippets of background from the profiles Betty had asked us to fill out. These were designed to help us become acquainted with each other and to aid Betty in setting up those contacts in the Soviet Union who would best match our individual interests. Now we were all finally coming together, and as we crowded into Betty and Kurt's room, someone commented, "Well, we're here; we survived," and we all laughed, thinking back to two days of seemingly endless travel and weeks of waiting and wondering.

Betty began our meeting by asking for volunteers to be "Worrier of the Day" or WOD, and "Scribe of the Day" or SOD. The WOD's job was to keep track of all the day's details, such as the times of scheduled events and the names of those attending, and handle logistics on traveling days so that Betty could concentrate on making arrangements with our tour guides and the people we would meet. The SOD's job was to keep a journal of the day's events —whom we met, what was said, where we went, and our reactions to everything. Sarah, who normally worked as a secretary, volunteered to be our SOD, and her daughter, Gert, an English teacher, took on our group "worries." Betty handed them notebooks, and then asked all of us to introduce ourselves and briefly tell what brought us here and what we hoped to accomplish on this trip.

Sarah began. "I've been a secretary for twenty years. My parents were born in the Ukraine, and I want to learn about my roots."

For Gert, the trip was a chance to practice speaking Russian, and, like her mother, she felt drawn to discovering more about her Ukranian heritage, which they would explore in Kiev.

Helga, an artist, was especially interested in meeting Russian artists. Recently she had hosted a group of Soviets, sponsored by her church, in her home. "I think there's so much misunderstanding between our countries; I want to bring the knowledge we gain back to people in my community, and I'd like to help the Soviets understand us better." She pulled out a folder of photographs she had taken of her home and community "to show them what everyday life in America is like."

Her daughter, Luci, also an artist, echoed her mother's comments about furthering more understanding, and also had some photos to share with Soviets.

For Angela, a city manager, the trip was about meeting ordinary Soviets face to face. "When our town hosted a group from the Soviet Union, I was very excited. But most of the Soviets I met represented some official organization. One was editor of a woman's magazine and another was high up in the Soviet Peace Committee. I felt I was hearing the party line and would rather have talked to these people just as *people*. I thought this trip would be a chance to do that—to walk down the street and talk to whomever we encounter."

Mike and his wife, Rowenna, both elementary schoolteachers, had had a tremendously moving experience when they volunteered to host Soviets in their home, Mike explained. "We offered to put up Alex and Oleg in our trailer, and it turned out to be a powerful, emotional experience, for through them we really saw the heart of the Russian people. Even my little daughter felt it." He motioned toward his three-year-old daughter, Belinda, sitting quietly on a pillow on the floor. "One night we couldn't find her, and when we went out to the trailer, there she was sitting on Alex's lap with her arms around his shoulders. I felt this powerful feeling of love, something I'd never felt for another man, an instant unspoken connection, for Alex didn't speak English. Then Alex said, as Oleg translated: 'We hope you will come to our country and bring your family.' Rowenna felt this love and sense of connection as well. We hope to see Alex and Oleg, and we want to meet more Soviet people."

Rowenna confided that it seemed as if some mystical calling had brought them. Even if they hadn't met Alex, she felt they eventually would have been drawn to the Soviet Union because of her peace work. "I organize a monthly program on peace and world issues, and it was natural to go to the Soviet Union because of my work. Also, I wanted to bring my children. It's crucial that they meet other children and develop this understanding, too."

Her older daughter, nine-year-old Darla, agreed. She pulled out some colorful cards and yarn bracelets she was making to give away. "They're peace cards and friendship bracelets."

Carolyn hoped to do her part in contributing to this time of historic change. She had done missionary work, and for her this trip was a kind of mission. "We need to do something to disperse the fear many people have about the Soviet Union. If we begin to *know* them, I think people would feel horrified at the idea of using weapons against them."

Jennifer had started writing a novel about a woman who goes to the Soviet Union, in part as an answer to her husband and teenage daughters who held more conventional views about

Soviets. "We had several discussions, actually more like fights, about what it's really like. Finally my husband said, 'Why don't you go and see for yourself?' So here I am."

Susan, a psychologist and counselor, came as a result of her own inner journey. "I've been exploring the psychology of higher consciousness for years, and when I met a group of Soviets who came to our school, something clicked. It was like seeing another side to ourselves. I suddenly saw how much we have to teach each other! We can learn from the Soviets—their values, some aspects of their system, and there are areas where we can bring them more up to date. It's as if our two countries are major parts to the world puzzle—we see how we might fit together now."

Charles, Susan's boyfriend, worked with computers. He hoped to meet Soviet programmers, and also get "a feel of what it's like to live in the Soviet Union."

Bill and Charity were retired, and described their work with several peace organizations. Bill was adamant that it was necessary to go beyond nationalism. "It's an outdated concept, and we're here to help move this world toward 'one world.' We want to talk with Soviets individually about how to achieve this."

I shared my hope that the *Glasnost* game I had created would stimulate the kinds of dialogue we had all been talking about, and then briefly described my plans to write this book. "It's designed to explain citizen diplomacy and promote mutual understanding."

Finally, all eyes turned toward our leaders, Kurt and Betty. What were their purposes in being here, and what did they envision for our trip?

Kurt waxed philosophical. "For me this trip represents a change in consciousness. I think the key event of the second half of the twentieth century will be the coming together of the United States and the U.S.S.R., and travelers such as ourselves are an important ingredient." He mentioned how he had seen his wife go off to the Soviet Union many times. "I lived these trips vicariously at first. Now I want to join in and work on creating exchange programs, especially with teachers."

Betty's life had been changed five years ago when she heard a recovered alcoholic describe his experience of helping people in the Soviet Union overcome their addiction. "I knew right then I wanted to do something, to act as a bridge to another culture as this man had done. On my first trip, the people I met were so warm—they radiated such a loving spirit. I felt the same kind of connection Mike and Rowenna described, and my life has never been the same."

Betty finished up the meeting with some last-minute reminders. It was important to follow the rules once we arrived, even if we felt some of them to be petty or unnecessary. Also, we had been briefed in our handouts—some real no-nos were black market involvement and sexual contact with a Soviet. We could get ourselves, the people we met, or the entire group in trouble.

In asking questions or responding to them, we were urged to recognize the differing conceptions of a good society, and be respectful.

We were urged to recognize and appreciate what works in the Soviet Union (such as child care, education, the subway system, and the low cost and extensive cultural activities) rather than notice only those things that didn't work or that we judged by our own consumer or democratic standards (such as the small standardized apartments and housing shortage, the scarcity of quality consumer goods, the harsh treatment of political dissidents, and the restrictions on traveling outside the Soviet Union). In short, to communicate successfully, we should feel free to acknowledge differences, but we should look for similarities to create a common basis for communication.

We were given some tips by Betty about going through customs, and even prepared for possible questioning about the items we would be bringing in. "The Soviets want to be sure we aren't planning to engage in black market dealings. If you're asked about anything, just explain it's a gift, and usually that will be all you need to say." Even if customs agents confiscated excess items at the border, we could get them back when we left. And if we didn't leave by the same city? Betty seemed to think everything would get sorted out. "In any case," she emphasized, "customs checks usually are not a problem. Normally they don't take anything and we sail right through."

She had a few comments about encounters we might have on the street. "You may find that mostly young people will approach you. Often they'll be involved in the black market, but others may just want to trade. Usually they will strike up a casual conversation first, so it's a good idea to carry buttons or other small gifts in your pockets which you can use for trading. However, if the person starts asking you about exchanging money, then it's best to move away."

She pointed out that the metros were an especially good place to meet people. Because the escalator rides lasted several minutes, there was plenty of time to talk to someone. Good conversation starters included asking for directions, or saying something like: "I'm an American—here's a token of peace and friendship." Then we might give a small button, pin, or post-card. Soviets liked receiving American mementos.

Betty closed by suggesting that a purpose for our particular trip could be "to support the Soviets as they go through this painful period of change." She felt enthusiastic about the recent changes that made it so much easier to connect with people. "There used to be so many restrictions on Soviets meeting foreigners, but now we can invite our Soviet friends to our hotel, and Soviets can feel freer to invite us to their homes."

In our first city, Leningrad, we would have an Intourist guide assigned who would stay with us for the entire trip. In addition, we would have guides in each city who would take care of local touring, and hotel and meal arrangements. While much would be planned, Betty said we could feel free to go off on our own, simply skipping a prearranged event and doing what we wanted.

"Feel free to improvise, within the rules. Since our goal is to meet the people, meet as many as you can. If you encounter people who want to meet more Americans, get their names and we'll add them to our list of contacts for future trips. This way, the network and connections will grow. You may think this trip will end in two weeks, but I assure you, it will continue on and on. In you and the people you meet."

A key part of this trip would be not only the diplomacy we established with the Soviets but also the close relationships we developed with our co-travelers. Certainly, I had been on other group trips where people got to know each other quite well by the end. But on this trip we might expect our relationships to be different, not only because we were going to a different culture but also because of our special mission as citizen diplomats.

This was to be a journey from the heart, to the heart; it would be about close feeling, close sharing, common hope, commitment to creating a better way of living on our fragile planet. Our group would become "family" and our hope would be to promote the development of a more cohesive world family.

The following pages describe this journey, which was to change all our lives. As one woman on the trip later described it: "This isn't just a journey to see the Soviet Union. It's a journey into ourselves."

PART II
LENINGRAD
The First Connections

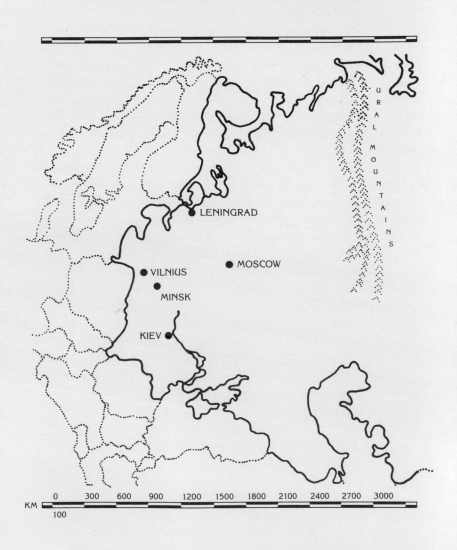

LENINGRAD

● MOSCOW

● VILNIUS

MINSK

KIEV

U R A L   M O U N T A I N S

KM

0   300   600   900   1200   1500   1800   2100   2400   2700   3000

100

CHAPTER 2

Finding Our Way Around

From Helsinki we arrived at the Leningrad airport under a bright, 11:00 A.M. sun, and despite dire warnings about customs, we breezed right through. Friends had cautioned me about grim-faced agents who would probably conduct a lengthy search of our bags, and with my portable typewriter, expensive camera, and oversized suitcases containing *Glasnost* games, books, and hundreds of metal buttons, I thought surely I'd be given a thorough check. But it didn't happen that way.

First we went through Passport Control. I pushed into the thin passage and stood before an agent in a booth who glanced back and forth at me and my picture as I gazed at his khaki-colored uniform tinged with bright red epaulets. With a quick punch of his stamp, he nodded and waved me on to customs, where I piled up my luggage and faced a slightly bored-looking agent who had just a hint of a smile. He simply motioned me through, merely glancing at my camera, which was supposed to go through the X-ray. Perhaps he was accommodating me because the Soviets use the older X-ray machines, which are more likely to adversely affect film.

Similarly, the others in our group sailed through quickly. Because Soviet customs is usually quite thorough, it was as if, in the spirit of *glasnost*, even the customs agents had put on a new face and were making it easier for the growing crush of

17

travelers to arrive in the U.S.S.R. I felt it to be a propitious sign for our journey.

But where was our guide? As we glanced around the bustling terminal where hundreds of travelers walked briskly by, no one seemed to be looking for us. Outside, there was no Intourist bus in sight. We couldn't take just any bus or taxi to our hotel because we didn't know which hotel it was; Intourist usually worked out these assignments at the last minute and would then inform the guide.

As our group waited outside, Betty and Kurt went to the Intourist desk (one is located in every airport to handle foreign travelers) to search out our guide. It was a little unnerving being so helpless until someone from Intourist could tell us what to do, and I think we all felt the tremendous power of this one organization. The clerk, however, was reassuring. "Don't worry," he said, "a bus is on its way. Intourist knew you were arriving; they just weren't sure when."

Our travel agent in the U.S. had sent a telex announcing our time of arrival, but as we were to discover, travel arrangements in the Soviet Union sometimes can seem like a mystery. At times we would find ourselves struggling with miscommunications, incorrectly issued tickets, flight delays, and assorted changes. It was best simply to relax and go with the flow.

Our hotel turned out to be the Prebaltiskaya, one of the largest in the Soviet Union, located on the Gulf of Finland. It was situated at the end of a long wide street. As we drew closer, we passed row upon row of typical Soviet apartment buildings—plain, concrete structures with rows of identical windows. Down one street I glimpsed the tip of a crane and scaffolding, indicating that even more construction was going on.

The Prebaltiskaya, like many Soviet hotels, resembled a huge, imposing fortress. It sat on a small rise, with two wings jutting out on either side so that it formed, along with its thousands of windows, a graceful concrete and glass arc overlooking a broad concrete plaza and a series of long, sweeping steps that cascaded down the hill.

Inside, we gathered at the check-in desk and traded our passports and visas for room keys. Though we were all sharing rooms, we received only one key that we were to turn in at the desk whenever we went out. And if we lost it?

"Don't," Betty cautioned us. This wasn't like an American hotel where we could easily get new keys. We might expect the group to be delayed while the hotel checked into the missing key, perhaps even searching our luggage, with the most likely result being required to pay for a new key, and perhaps even a small fine. It seemed keys were as important as some of the documents we carried.

Our rooms consisted of two thin single beds with simple linen spreads, a black-and-white T.V. tucked into a dark wooden cabinet, an adjoining small bathroom with a few white and floral-patterned towels draped over a towel rack, and a bathtub with a hose and showerhead leading up from the faucets to the top of a stand. By American standards this room might be considered very small and simple, but by Soviet standards it was representative of a first-class hotel. It provided my roommate, Jennifer, and me the first occasion of many not to judge with "American eyes."

We had a few minutes to freshen up before going to lunch in one of the half-dozen restaurants in the hotel. As was the usual practice, a few tables had been set aside for our group, and we could plan on being served there every day at a time set by our guide.

Meals were generally worked out in advance. We could make individual requests such as vegetarian meals, which featured fish and chicken or extra vegetables instead of red meats, but once set, the hotel normally wouldn't make any variations. Our first meal in the Soviet Union, a typically full and hearty lunch, consisted of smoked salmon hors d'oeuvres, white and brown bread, vegetable soup, either sliced beef or fried chicken with potatoes and sauerkraut, rich coffee or tea, Pepsi Cola, and ice cream for dessert. The main meal is served at lunchtime, although dinner is almost as large, just a course or two less.

After lunch our guide, Lena, finally arrived. She would be with us for nearly our entire trip; her first suggestion was that this might be a good time to show us the metro—the heart of the Leningrad transportaion system. Normally such a tour in the middle of rush hour would be unheard of, but Lena thought it would be especially useful for us, because we wanted to learn how to get around on our own and to meet people. Other, more traditional Intourist guides probably wouldn't have attempted this—what if one of us got lost in the crush?—but as we were soon to learn, Lena was not the traditional Intourist guide. One of the younger guides, she turned out to be innovative, flexible, and immediately receptive to our special purpose in visiting the U.S.S.R.

So it was decided. We agreed to meet in front of the hotel in fifteen minutes and head for the metro. Meanwhile, in the short time we had, a few of us went to the money exchange in the hotel. Because the exchange rate is the same everywhere in the Soviet Union (there is only one state-controlled bank), it didn't matter where we changed our money as long as we didn't exchange with someone who approached us on the street, since such private exchanges were considered illegal. We had to have our customs forms with us as well, so that the officials could keep track of our money and make sure we weren't engaging in illegal dealing.

This exchange took only a few minutes. The clerk noted the source of the funds I was using to change into rubles. This notation was important because it's possible to change rubles back into dollars if you have changed them from dollars, but not if you have used a credit card. If you use traveler's checks to obtain rubles there's an extra commission for conversion added on.

After I rejoined the group, Lena led us to the bus stop. She had advised us to buy a book of ten tickets (for fifty kopeks) at our hotel, which would be easier than trying to buy them on the bus from the driver. Lena had her own tickets in case we didn't have them, and these were punched by a small machine near the rear door of the bus. Then we kept the punched tickets. It was important to hold on to these because occasionally someone from the system would check them.

"If you don't have your ticket there's a three-ruble fine, payable on the spot," one Soviet later explained to me. However, people tended to be quite honest. In fact, if the bus was crowded, people might pass their ticket from hand to hand across the bus, and their punched tickets would be returned the same way.

"Does anyone ever pocket the tickets?" I asked my Soviet acquaintance.

"Of course not," he replied, looking at me incredulously. "No one would do such a thing. We operate on the honor system, you know."

While we were instructed to mount the bus through the back doors and work our way forward to fit in with the flow, people in fact seemed to pile on from everywhere, pushing their way out from either door creating a kind of free-for-all—much like riding buses in New York.

While some Americans might have found this pushing, elbowing behavior rude and unfriendly, just the opposite is true. Physical closeness is a cultural characteristic of the Soviets, unlike Americans who generally are brought up to keep a certain distance. So instead of complaining when we encountered crowds in buses, in the metro, and on busy streets, we followed the advice we received as part of our pre-trip preparation to work on adapting or blending in, and simply jostled and pushed right back. And, when we did, it was actually fun. There was something vital and enlivening about it.

Within minutes, we arrived at the metro station, a prominent circular building of concrete surmounted by a large *M*. The path to the metro led through a wide plaza where vendors sold such diverse items as magazines, newspapers, maps, souvenirs, trinkets, cosmetics, and plastic toys (one was a colorful little bird that peeped when squeezed). Several sold lottery or theater tickets; others served pastries, ice cream cones, and sodas. Rows of vending machines provided glasses of juice or water for five kopeks. People pushed and scrambled to get to these stalls, usually having to stand in line. Lena urged us on, so that we wouldn't get separated from the group.

The metro required a five-kopek coin, and as she had done on the bus, Lena supplied our fare this time if we didn't have our own kopeks. Because we would use them later, she showed us the change machines—small metal boxes lined up along the wall with flashing yellow lights to indicate they were working. I happened to notice a man hitting one of the machines. Lena saw me and smiled. "Well, sometimes the machines don't work." We all nodded in understanding.

Now it was time to jump into the current of rushing people. Lena guided us toward the open turnstiles where a patch of red light to the side was waiting to turn to green with the drop of our coin. It looked to me as if someone could go through anyway, since the passage was completely open. But as I pushed ahead, curious to see what would happen, I soon learned there was no easy way to trick the system. With a snap, a metal gate flew down in front of me. I quickly popped in my money.

Around us, crowds surged through these turnstiles like armies of ants, one surge leaving after being disgorged at the top of the escalators, another moving toward the escalators, which pointed down at a forty-five degree angle into what looked like a dark, endless tunnel. In seconds, we were being pushed along and sucked toward this tunnel, which reminded me of a big gaping mouth eager to be fed by the streams of people pouring toward it.

I barely heard Lena in the uproar, who was yelling something about meeting again at the bottom of the escalator. As it sped down all I could see was an unbroken flow of people. Lena advised us to stay to the right so that those in a hurry could clamber by on the left, and although the break-neck speed of the scurrying people and swift-moving escalator felt a bit scary to me, in time I would get used to being a part of it, even racing ahead myself as the Soviet metros became familiar territory.

Meanwhile, the Soviets around me who weren't rushing seemed completely relaxed. They whizzed by in the opposite direction casually reading books, or calmly facing each other and talking as if they had all the time in the world. And, in fact, it took several minutes even at high speed to get to the bottom, where we boarded yet another escalator that took us deeper still.

When we reached our destination I looked around in amazement. The platform was spacious with broad arching columns. The marble and ceramic tile walls were spotless, and as the trains pulled in, their steely blue cars glistened. It was as if someone had just washed down the station for an inspection, and it stood in stark contrast to the graffiti and grime in the subway stations I usually tried to avoid in New York.

I remarked on the differences, and how safe I felt, as we waited for everyone in our group to arrive. Lena simply replied, as if having heard this many times, "Our metro has no graffiti because no one would think of doing such a thing. It would be an offense to the state and harshly punished. Because the metro is appreciated as something for all the people, no one would want to deface it."

The metro was also quite safe because it was usually crowded at all times, even late at night until it stopped running at 1:00 A.M., and there were no dangerous roving gangs. But we had to get used to the rush, the snapping doors, and bullet-fast cars, and there was some assurance in knowing that every three minutes there would be another one.

Now that everyone was assembled, we threw ourselves into the racing throng and onto the train, some of us dropping down into the few empty seats. The car whooshed away. Ten minutes later we were in downtown Leningrad.

"Now out quickly," Lena cried, and, as on the bus, we pushed and elbowed our way through the crowd and out the door.

At the end of our escalator ride we were rewarded with arriving at the large boulevard called the Nevsky Prospect, running through the heart of downtown Leningrad. Here pulsed the same fast-paced energy as throngs of people swept by, and I was again reminded of New York. Looking around, however, I started noticing differences. Most obvious was the clothing. Any one person might look right at home in a modern U.S. city, but overall, the streets had a more casual, homey feel, as if, instead of getting dressed up to go out, people went out in what they also wore around the house. Few men were wearing crisp business suits, and few women wore the suits, skirts, and starched blouses that generally signify business success. Rather, most of the women had donned simple, shirtwaist-style dresses, many with flower prints, and only a few (mostly the younger generation) were wearing slacks. The men were attired in casual open-collared shirts and slacks, and some of the younger men sported jeans.

Lena led us into one of the underground passageways, the usual way to cross a busy central street. Old women were selling their wares at either end. When we emerged, we saw shops in all directions, and Lena invited us to explore the city on our own for a while.

I started walking, wanting to throw myself into the feel of Leningrad, imagining what it would be like to live here every day. I began to pick up the rhythms and moods all around me. There was a lively contrast between the bustling crowds and the patient lines of people pressed up against each other like beads on a chain as they waited in front of the small vending tables and kiosks that popped up every few hundred yards along the sidewalk. At the tables where there were no lines, people strategically moved in, pressed their money on the vendor, took their purchases and left quickly—like football players scoring touchdowns.

A few women, and even a few men, walked arm in arm or held hands, again reminding me how Soviets openly express their feelings of companionship, friendship, and affection without the sexual associations we might assign to such behavior. From time to time, we frequently saw men and women kissing or hugging in public—but this didn't mean that a same-sex couple was gay or that a heterosexual pair was having an affair. They were just expressing their mutual caring in a friendly way.

The vendors brought something of a carnival flavor to the street. They hawked small impulse items—decals, jewelry, scarves—generally costing less than a ruble and easier to pick up here than in a store. I noticed that people brought their own shopping bags for these chance encounters. I pushed forward through one knot of people to see a man demonstrating a small device. He spoke with the excitement of the carnival pitchman as he held up this marvelous tool and demonstrated how, with just a flick of his wrist, it could fix a stocking so it wouldn't run. The women gasped with amazement and hastily pressed their rubles on him.

Further down the street, a group of artists had set up a gallery of their works, featuring snow-covered country scenes, glimpses of city streets, and portraits of clowns, dogs, and cats. Other artists had set up easels and invited passersby to pose. It all reminded me of the streets of Greenwich Village.

I later learned that, while most of the vendors were employed by the state and the small stands had been part of the street scene for years, these artists represented a new wave of small-scale entrepreneurship unleashed by the spirit of *glasnost*. More and more people now were earning money by making and selling small crafts.

I visited a number of indoor specialty shops. Typically in Soviet cities these occupy the ground floor of buildings that house offices or apartments and present a sharp contrast to department stores, which have their own buildings. The department stores pulsed to a kind of noisy, staccato beat as people surged up and down stairs, angled for places at counters, or waited in long lines. But the specialty shops felt vast and cavernous, with few customers and few products. Quiet, almost restful, they provided a welcome relief to the crowds, and in some places I felt as though I were entering a museum or gallery. One fabric store presented a spectrum of color in material arranged in sprays against the walls, and a tie store had laid out its merchandise like spokes in a series of colorful wheels.

As I wandered, drawing myself deeper and deeper into this nerve center of Soviet life, I thought about these people we had traveled so far to meet face to face. It was true they didn't smile as much as Americans, who often walk around with a smile no matter how they feel. This did not mean the Soviets were unhappy, cold, or calculating, as sometimes portrayed in the media. Rather, as I was to discover later when I met them in their homes, the Soviets are an extremely warm, expressive, generous, and loving people behind their more reserved public exterior.

Suddenly on the street I encountered Luci and Helga who had just come from visiting the big bookstore called the Dom Kniga, or House of Books. Luci pulled out an illustrated book on Leningrad, when suddenly two men appeared beside us. They were young, in their twenties, and looked quite ordinary in their slacks and open shirts.

"Would you like to change some money?" one of them said to Luci, glancing at her book in English, the sure sign of a tourist.

"We can offer you two rubles for the dollar," the other chimed in. "It's better than the official rate." We weren't sure what to do. Luci shook her head. "No, I can't do that."

"Well, we can make it four to one," said the first, keeping up with our quick pace. When Luci again said no, the two men peeled away. Over the next two weeks we would have many such black market encounters, and I would come to understand the reasons for the strong antiblack-market feelings among the people here.

For now, we left the black marketeers behind us and walked the few blocks to our bus. Lena wanted to take us to a *beryozka* store, and it proved to be a fitting conclusion to our educational outing. *Beryozkas* are foreign (or hard) currency stores that carry goods mostly unavailable in regular Soviet stores and at lower prices. This is because hard currency has a higher value on the international monetary market than the ruble. Soviets normally are not allowed to shop in the *beryozkas*. Even if they could afford the items, they are not supposed to have dollars, the assumption being that if they did, they would most certainly have procured them on the black market.

I couldn't help wondering if the Soviets didn't feel a little envious of the foreigners' ability to purchase these luxurious goods priced as much as one-third higher in the Soviet stores, or not sold there at all. Stepping into the *beryozka* was like entering a paradise for tourists. In addition to lavish books about art and Soviet cities, there were specialty items such as Russian furs, amber and gold jewelry, vodka, and caviar plentifully displayed, as well as traditional folk-crafted souvenirs such as colorful nesting dolls and exquisite black lacquer boxes. We could use cash, traveler's checks, and credit cards to buy expensive recorders, cameras, and kitchen appliances, which were generally out of the reach of most Soviets.

On the way back to the hotel I felt bothered by this system of separate stores—it didn't seem quite fair. Why couldn't the Soviets just use any dollars they might have to shop here? But Lena reminded me of all that the government subsidizes for the people—housing, education, food, travel.

We were to learn later when we grew to know the people more personally that Soviets consider the lack of consumer goods available to the average citizen a key problem in their society. Thus, they might think up creative ways to gain access to the *beryozka* goods or ask their American or other foreign friends to help them acquire these valued, modern-day items. There also existed the temptation of the black market. I felt the deep dilemma inherent in these issues and wondered what answers might lie ahead.

CHAPTER 3

Making Our First Connections

At dinner Betty informed us that Ursula, the daughter of a friend of her Russian teacher in the U.S. (this is called networking!) was eager to meet us. She had arranged to be on the steps of our hotel that evening to greet those of us who would like to come. Fortunately, both Gert and Jennifer, who spoke Russian, volunteered to join the group, as did Betty, Kurt, Sarah, and I. We were meeting her outside on the steps because Ursula was nervous about coming inside, apprehensive that the doorman might stop and question her. Possibly these were memories of the old rules operating, because most of the Soviets we met felt free to come into the hotels as our guests, and normally they breezed right through.

At 10:00 P.M. we gathered on the steps to wait for Ursula, and after fifteen minutes had passed, we began to be concerned since Soviets are usually quite prompt. Suddenly I noticed a woman of about forty standing in the center of the hotel plaza, and it turned out to be Ursula. We exchanged hellos and *dobry dyehns* (Russian for good evening).

Since Ursula obviously felt more comfortable away from the hotel, we started walking down the street towards the Baltic. The conversation was slow and tedious. Sometimes Ursula understood our English, and sometimes she didn't. Gert or Jennifer usually broke in to translate, but at times they would forget. However, despite the language barrier, something amazing was taking place. A bond of friendship was developing, a bridge of feeling that transcended our communication difficulties. Somehow, the desire to build that bridge of friendship was stronger than mere words.

Ursula said that she and her roommate, Olga, also a teacher like herself, would like us to come to dinner the next evening. As if to emphasize this, Ursula suddenly pulled a box of chocolates from her bag and passed them around as we stood on a walkway near the Baltic. "Please, take," she said, and we each took one. They were filled with rum and had a pleasant tingling sensation. Sarah pulled out a peace button with a blue dove on it and pinned it on Ursula's sweater. I handed her one of my *Glasnost* buttons while Gert explained it as the symbol for my game about how Americans and Soviets might work together for peace.

"Oh, we must all play this tomorrow night," Ursula beamed.

I couldn't imagine how we could all play this, since we could all barely communicate, but I just nodded. "Of course, I'll bring it," I said. At the time I wasn't even sure I wanted to go, since I found our communication so slow and stilted. But since the others were so enthusiastic, and there was such an atmosphere of genuine warmth, I put my reservations aside and instead contemplated the rare opportunity of visiting a Soviet home. Later, as we walked Ursula to her bus amidst the gloam of Leningrad's "white night"—it was just starting to get dark around 11:30—I asked Betty if Ursula's friend would be any more proficient in English.

"Oh, no," Betty said, smiling broadly and apparently not at all concerned by our language hurdles. "This is as good as it gets."

As we waited for Ursula's bus, I noticed a man nodding off inside the small wooden bus shelter. His head bobbed up and down a few times, then fell on his chest. A few minutes later, a police van pulled up and two men in blue uniforms with red patches got out. They gently jostled the man awake, led him to the van, and drove off, all within the span of a minute. The man didn't struggle or try to resist, and I marveled at the speed, ease, and silence of this whole process.

Ursula explained that the police were part of a patrol to keep drunk people off the streets, especially around the tourist hotels. They would probably release him tomorrow or keep him longer if this was a repeated offense. The effort was less an attempt at punishment than one of rehabilitation, and Ursula felt it was working because there were fewer cases of drunkenness and less crime on the streets (most crimes are committed by alcoholics). Of course, this may have been helped by the fact that there was less alcohol available than formerly. An active public education campaign urging people not to drink had been launched. Many of the shops that sold liquor had either shut down or had shortened their hours, and the price of alcohol had gone up.

There was, however, a growing problem of people making their own alcohol, this moonshine production causing a sugar shortage—shades of our own era of prohibition and bathtub gin? One result of this increase in alcohol use at home was that kids were now beginning to drink earlier in life, a distressing fact in a culture where children and their education are highly valued. Still, Ursula and others we talked to supported the campaign. They liked the fact that they saw fewer inebriated people sleeping in their streets or huddled in doorways, as in times past.

The morning began with a meeting designed to bring us all together again as a group and help us reaffirm our purpose. Betty began with a brief nondenominational prayer called "A Blessing Prayer When About to Leave on a Journey." We all crowded together in her hotel room as she quietly read the words:

Blessed are you, God our creator, for this wide and wonderful world in which we can travel.

We ask your blessings upon us as we are about to leave on this journey.

Be our ever-near companion and spread the road before us with beauty and adventure.

On this trip may we take with us as part of our traveling equipment,

A heart wrapped in wonder with which to rejoice in all that we shall meet.

May your blessing be upon us throughout this trip,

And bring us home again in safety and peace.

Betty then prepared us for our first city tour with a brief history of the U.S.S.R. A small dose of Soviet history goes a long way toward understanding the people themselves. Soviets are immersed in their history—geographically and psychologically. "We live with our history all around us," Lena would tell us later, "and we hope our children will have this sense of history, too. They need to understand what we have been through, so it does not happen again."

Centuries of feudalism and brutal invasions characterize their historical landscape. In Tsarist Russia, which began in the fifteenth century, they lived in an absolute monarchy with the Tsar as dictator. While the English nobles in the West were enjoying basic freedoms granted to them by the Magna Carta of 1215, even upper class landowners (called *boyars*) were under the Tsar's firm thumb, and he repeatedly used oppressive measures, including arbitrary arrest and imprisonment, forced labor, secret police, thought control, and ruthless repression of any resistance, to keep them in line.

When the Communist Party took over in 1917, it was able to continue enforcing such measures on a people already used to strong central control. Thus, even while modernizing his country, Stalin ruled with an iron hand, crushing dissent with his horrifying purges. Worst of all was Hitler's invasion in World War II, which left over 20 million dead, two-thirds of the entire country in ruin, and over 25 million homeless.

As we began our tour, it was easy to see that this suffering and oppression seemed etched in Lena's memory. The fear, hunger, and devastation of war, particularly of Leningrad during World War II, seemed to live inside her as she spoke—but so did the spirit of hope. Out of this shocking history had come much rebuilding, and there was great pride in her voice as she pointed to the many buildings and squares dedicated to the memory of her people's honor—this one built in the seventeenth century by Peter the Great, that one in the eighteenth by Catherine the Great, this statue in honor of the heroes of the Revolution, that one to celebrate the success of the Bolsheviks. Living in Leningrad was like living in a museum where every place had its own history. As we rode, a panoply of Russian history unfolded before us, from the days of the warring tribes, to the building of the czarist empire, to the transformation of the Revolution, to the great changes taking place today.

I thought about Soviet and American differences. The Soviets are so concerned to preserve and remember, while Americans seemed more apt to tear down and forget, eager to move on to the new in the name of progress. Do we sometimes fail to appreciate our past? On the other hand, does this makes us more free to shape the future? We have been born of optimism and energy, with the conviction that all will turn out for the best in the name of freedom. We smile and have such hope, contrasted with the image of the more serious, thoughtful Soviet. Our very different histories have shaped us. Americans haven't experienced repeated invasions and wars on our land; we haven't been occupied, conquered. Instead, we have often been the conquerers.

The Field of Mars Square, dedicated to those killed in the three revolutions—in 1905, and in February and October of 1917—seemed to fill the bus windows. Next came the Winter Palace, or Hermitage, built for the czars and nearly destroyed during World War II. "We want people to understand," Lena said. "We feel we are not believed when we say we want peace. But if you will look around you, you will see how much we do."

After lunch we had the opportunity to meet with a Soviet writer to learn his feelings about current topics and the changes going on within the government. Up until recently most Soviets would not have felt free to speak in a public place or to share feelings and opinions openly with people they had just met. Yet here was Viktor unself-consciously sharing his perspectives with a dozen Americans in a rear lobby of our hotel. This more open communication was part of the new spirit of change sweeping through the Soviet Union, and Viktor saluted the opening of this door. "At least it's open for now," he stated. "We hope it stays open."

We had many questions, and Viktor began by speaking on the ecological problems now facing the Soviet Union. He was part of an active group of about fifty people, mostly in their twenties and thirties, who had formed a "non-official" movement to clean up the environment. They held meetings a few times a month and occasionally planned demonstrations. "We must educate people," he said, and explained how his group was working to draw attention to the factories spilling pollution into the Baltic Sea around Leningrad.

He asked us for ideas on how to disseminate information, and I realized how much more difficult it was to organize a popular movement here calling attention to social problems. The formation of these organizations flew in the face of the people's trust in their system, which followed a tradition of waiting for and then acquiescing to whatever the state officials decided. In addition, on a more practical level, it is extremely difficult to dispense information in a system where all the copy machines belong to the state. At the time of our visit, access to computers, typewriters, and printing presses was sporadic and

limited, resulting in the following "system" among people organizing for change: They would type up multiple carbon copies of an item, then pass the copies around!

Still, Viktor was hopeful that their efforts counted and that
the movement was growing. He spent most of his free time on
it.

Charity, who was active in the Beyond War movement, wanted
to know what Viktor and other Soviets thought we might do to
encourage more friendship between our two nations. "Many of
us feel our government isn't doing enough," she said.

Viktor felt it was up to the people themselves. As he put it:
"Friendship is only possible among people, not between countries and organizations, for only people have feelings. In fact,
countries and organizations can create obstructions. If you like
the people you meet from another country, then you'll feel the
country is okay. I feel it's important for individuals in our countries to have more personal, positive experiences with each
other—as we are doing now."

Later, I heard many other Soviets echo this theme—talk to
the people, not to the bureaucrats who have to present the
official view. Make your connections one-on-one, share feelings, touch hearts. These were the sentiments of the ordinary
Soviet people we met who wanted to see their society open up
and change.

Susan reminded us all at this point about the Party Congress currently going on in Moscow, and asked Viktor how he
and other Soviets felt about Gorbachev and the historic events
taking place.

"First of all, it is my view that people feel very positive about
the Congress because its agenda is to separate the functions of
the Party and government, and limit the Party's role." Viktor
saw the Party as ruling the country and emphasized his and
others' feelings that this should not be so. "The people should
elect representatives who govern on their behalf.

"Gorbachev came to power with an emphasis on human
faith. He believes in the power of the people, and that very belief

will help to empower everyone. When you have someone at the top who has plans and goals that include personal involvement and democratic freedom, then you have the key that inspires personal dedication and fulfillment, and motivates individuals in society to contribute to the whole. And the freer the better, because freedom generates the creativity needed to solve problems.

"The events taking place in our time are very important. During the Brezhnev years, we couldn't talk openly. But now people feel free to express their views. Even our press is beginning to speak frankly without fear of punishment. This openness helps connect us to each other in new ways—within our society, with others, with you."

Viktor's words were strong, yet also gentle somehow, as if he were reassuring us. There was something in the air—a new beginning? A world where we might all learn to live together?

"We are planting seeds," Viktor picked up my thoughts. "Meeting as we are now, and promoting more personal stories and images in the media, we are cultivating a garden of peace. As it spreads, it will cut off the roots of war."

Our dinner gathering that evening with Ursula and Olga also had the feeling of breaking ground. In the past these visits were somewhat risky although it was not illegal for Soviets to have foreigners in their apartments. There might be questions, suspicions. "Why do you have Americans in your home?" someone from the neighborhood committee might ask. "Are you dissatisfied about something?" From then on there might be KGB-types watching and listening. Because few Soviets wanted to go through this kind of scrutiny, they previously tended to avoid such contacts.

Now, seven of us were wending our way to the far ends of the metro—for Ursula and Olga lived at the end of the line—

and as we pulled into the station, we perceived that it must be Olga who was was eagerly waiting for us on the platform.

We were half an hour late, most likely a common phenom- enon among metro initiates, and must have been easy to spot as we clustered together on the platform looking lost. Olga greeted us profusely. A small, squat bundle of energy with a cap of red hair, she made a beeline toward us and extended her hands in a gesture of welcome. "I am Olga," she cried. "You have come!"

Betty greeted her, then quite spontaneously they hugged, and Olga led us to the escalator for the long ride up to the street.

We were greeted by a suburb of Leningrad, relatively new and typical of the outlying areas of large Soviet cities. Blocks of tall apartment buildings fanned out in every direction, and along with the metro, bus and trolley lines had followed this urban expansion like a web connecting everything to the center. Olga led us across a wide main street, down a rutted dirt path between two tall buildings, then along a narrow paved road that passed by a volleyball court. Two teams of men were playing, and a few women wearing flowered shirtwaist dresses wheeled baby carriages nearby.

On the way, in bits of English and with the help of Gert and Jennifer, Olga talked about their home, saying we would find it typical in its small size and simple furnishings. "It is unusual that only two people live there now because at one time it housed three families. Now the others have moved out, and I'm staying there only temporarily."

We arrived at the building, an older, squarish structure that had been there before the new wave of taller tenements had taken over. The door was unlocked, and we ascended the three flights of stairs through a dark and musty stairwell; apparently, the light had burned out. Olga explained that the older build- ings with less than six floors generally did not have elevators.

Ursula was waiting at the top of the stairs to greet us. We removed our shoes and entered the cozy living room where she had set up a long table and several straight-back chairs. There was a flowered couch, a low coffee table made of dark wood, and a small television in a wooden cabinet. On plain white walls hung a few pictures of Russian country scenes and shelves with dolls, embossed glasses, and flowered boxes.

"Please sit," Ursula commanded, and retreated into the kitchen just off the living/dining room area. "We'll be ready in a minute."

As she and Olga bustled about, I noticed their kitchen looked somewhat like a typical American kitchen of the fifties, with its small, boxy refrigerator, white sink and gas stove, and speckled linoleum floor. There was limited space and none of the modern appliances so common in American kitchens such as a dishwasher, automatic coffee maker, or blender.

"Please feel free to look around," Ursula called from the kitchen as if sensing what we were all thinking. We went down a hallway off of which were three bedrooms, lined up one after the other, each containing a narrow bed with a colorful spread, a wooden bureau, and a sprinkling of pictures and books. Ursula's room also had a maple desk and a bookshelf filled with dozens of paperbacks in Russian.

At the end of the hall was the bathroom, about six feet square with the fixtures pushed close together. The shower had a thin plastic curtain and a hose leading up from the faucets to a shower head perched on a small ring.

I felt as if we were intruders, observing their apartment in somewhat the same way as we might visit a museum. I tried to imagine several people living here. My own apartment must have been twice this size, and I realized how much I valued the space I had, and took it for granted. Here people had learned to live much closer together, seemingly giving up much of their privacy. But many people told me later that living in cramped conditions actually offered them a feeling of closeness and connection with others that we often miss, with our emphasis on separateness and individualism.

Ursula and Olga appeared with the main course of our meal, and we sat down to a green salad piled high with lettuce and cucumbers and a heaping platter of rice pilaf with bits of lamb. We were urged to fill our plates, and when we were finished they brought out more, followed by a platter of three different deserts: baklava, cheesecake, and an assortment of cookies. Olga also brought in something considered a special treat—a large bowl of ripe black cherries she had purchased in the marketplace. Afterwards came a samovar of Russian tea that we sipped from small china cups.

The Russian approach to hospitality has a long tradition. People entertain guests in their homes rather than going out to dinner, and they prepare sumptuous meals, taking pride in their ability to cook. In addition, Ursula had spent long hours shopping to get the ingredients needed because Soviets don't have the convenience of a supermarket to get all their food in a single stop. She had to go to one shop for the vegetables, another for the meat, a third for the fresh black cherries, and still another for the bakery goods. It was a far cry from running down to the local deli and getting something to heat up.

We felt honored by their generosity, both in their culinary offerings and in their enthusiam to share their lives and views about the Soviet system. For the most part the conversation was in Russian, with Ursula and Olga moving their hands around in wide sweeping gestures and gazing at us intently as they spoke, as if they thought we understood what they were saying.

With Jennifer and Gert interjecting brief summations, Olga described her recent experiences as a teacher in Uzbeckestan, where she had left Leningrad five years ago to go because the pay was better. As an incentive to encourage people to go to outlying areas, the state would add ten percent per year to their earnings for up to five years. Olga hoped to use this extra money to get a better apartment or perhaps even a car. Now that her five years of extra earning potential were completed, she had returned to Leningrad and what she called "a much more cultural life."

However, Olga had to find a job before she could return permanently. The Soviet Union has an internal passport system, and until one's passport can be changed to show residency in a particular city, he or she cannot gain access to health care and other social services or arrange for a permanent apartment. Only with a letter of approval from a place of employment can these passports be changed.

To further complicate matters, Olga complained of the discrimination she encountered in her job search because she is Jewish. She felt that the better jobs were not available to Jews, and even worried about going to a synagogue for fear of losing her job once she found one.

This sparked a lively debate between the two of them, which fanned out to include a number of issues. Ursula, who was also Jewish, insisted that Olga was free to go to a synagogue without any reprisals, saying that many of the conditions of the past had been rectified. But Olga didn't want to take the chance and expressed a longing for the freedoms we enjoy in America. She explained that she had friends who had gone to live there, and though homesick for Leningrad, they did not want to return and face giving up their basic freedoms.

So did Olga dream of going to the United States? "Oh, no," she protested. "I like my country, the culture, the people. I just don't like the difficulties we sometimes face. We need more freedom to be ourselves—to be individuals."

Again Ursula disagreed. "No, no. Communism is good, much better for taking care of everyone as a whole," and then in Russian the two battled their different beliefs. What surprised me was that, despite their strong differences, they were still the closest of friends; in fact, their differences seemed to add a kind of good-humored spice to their relationship.

Because Olga was looking for employment, I asked her how people obtain their positions.

"Since most people work for the state, they go to special boards or bureaus to apply for state jobs," she replied. "The bureaus have records of what is available and assist anyone seeking a job for the first time, wanting a job change, or planning to move to a new city. When applying, it is necessary to show a diploma, but not a recommendation from a previous job. In some cases there may be an examination, with the person scoring highest getting the job. Once someone begins work at an enterprise, he or she can stay for as long as he wants."

"What if the enterprise needs fewer people? Wouldn't it have to let some employees go?"

"Not normally," Olga said. "If the enterprise finishes producing something, it would go on to create something new. The manager informs the state that it is nearing the end of a project and another assignment will be scheduled, so everyone is assured of a continuing job."

"Do people ever lose their job due to poor performance?"

"Not usually. It is difficult to fire anyone unless he is an alcoholic, takes drugs, or commits some serious crime. It's important in our system to keep everyone employed; however, if a person doesn't do his job well or repeatedly comes in late, the administration can lower his salary until he reforms. Conversely, if a person performs well, his pay might be increased for good work."

I learned that there was a job for everyone in the Soviet Union. They don't have unemployment insurance, for as Olga explained, they would not pay anyone to be out of work. If people need money for continuing education or retraining, they could apply for the social consumption funds, which the Soviet system maintains to help people with special needs. The government draws from social consumption funds to pay for each person's education and medical expenses, but the funds are also there for every kind of personal need involving money, including pregnancy leave, and rest and recuperation at a resort.

Those who wish to leave their jobs just inform their managers, and can generally be free within two weeks to go to one of the boards or bureaus to seek another job. However, some enterprises require an employee to sign on for a specific term. For example, after finishing college, a person agrees to stay at a job for three years, and after that time he can try for something else.

I asked about the tax system, explaining the sliding scale system in the U.S., and Olga said it was similar in the Soviet Union. "Usually workers pay about eight to thirteen percent of their salary, and if someone is in private practice or freelances, he also pays taxes in line with his earnings. For example, a craftsman who earns less than 840 rubles a year, or doctors and teachers who earn less than 300 rubles a year in their private practices, pay no tax. However, workers who make more than 1200 rubles a year pay a tax of thirty-three percent, and for those who make more than 7000 rubles, the tax is sixty-nine percent."

After dinner, we played my game. "Let's try out some *Glasnost*," Ursula said, and as the table was cleared I spread out the game.

The intricate guidelines for play are hard enough to explain briefly in English, but one by one I described the rules to Gert, and she explained them in Russian to Ursula and Olga who listened patiently. After about ten minutes they announced, "Let's play!" And somehow we did.

Part of the game features a series of questions designed to generate debate. Here's how it went: One of us picked up a card and read the question aloud in English. Gert translated, and as we answered, she translated again. It was admittedly not the best way to play the game, but it engendered some interesting dialogues. For example, when Gert read aloud, "Do you think the Soviet Union may be giving up communism or becoming more capitalistic as a result of the changes going on now?" Ursula broke in spiritedly. "I don't like that question because our definitions are different. You see, the Soviets define capitalism as exploiting the worker, but you see it as making money. So we are not becoming more 'capitalistic,' but we are encouraging people to make more money. They just have to make it the communist way; they can't hire people to work for them, for we consider that to be exploitation." Of course, Olga jumped in to take issue, and so it went.

We left about eleven o'clock, after hugs all around, and

Olga walked us to the station amidst the pink and blue hues of the evening. The volleyball players were still at their game, several people walked their dogs, and some teenagers tossed around a ball.

"Is this really night?" I felt as though it were the middle of the afternoon.

Olga smiled. "It's always light like this during the summer months. We have trouble thinking of this as night ourselves, and people stay up late. But since we do have to go to work in the morning, people will soon go to bed."

This was hard to imagine as we entered the metro, for it was jammed with people, and within minutes a train pulled up and whisked us away. Back at our hotel, the sky had turned a steely gray and the headlights of the passing buses and trolleys shimmered on the pavement. I felt a glow of satisfaction about the connection we had made this evening. Our differences had faded away, and the communion we had shared seemed to light the way for the days ahead.

CHAPTER 4

Law and Justice in the U.S.S.R.

In the morning Angela and I met Nina, a criminal defense attorney for fifteen years. Nina was a trim, bird-like woman of about forty, whose gray-flecked black hair gave her an air of authority. Attired in a plain blue skirt and blue-and-white short-sleeved blouse, and toting a thin briefcase, she was dressed much like she would be if appearing in court, where dress is slightly more informal than in the U.S. We rode the bus downtown to the courthouse, and on the way Nina answered our questions. First we discussed costs and fees, most of which are fairly standardized by the state. I was impressed by the low cost of justice for the average individual—about thirty rubles (equivalent to about fifty dollars) for a lawyer's services in handling a simple case such as petty theft or one person getting into a fight with another.

Such low fees, however, meant that lawyers ended up with relatively little. "Lawyers make, on an average, about 150 rubles (or about $250) a month," Nina explained. "Even factory workers doing hard labor generally make more. We receive a basic salary, then seventy-two percent of the client's fee—the rest is kept by the bar association. Sometimes lawyers can earn a little more if they acquire a good reputation and clients ask for them and are willing to pay a little more. But generally, lawyers earn relatively little."

In her own case, Nina had to do a lot for her twenty-two rubles. With each new client, she would go over the files, then travel to the jail or the home of the client to discuss the case. This might require several trips. Furthermore, if the case became difficult, there might be appeals. "Clients can give us extra rubles for all this work as a gift, and that is all right as long as the lawyer doesn't take the initiative and ask for it," Nina observed. "But if a lawyer says something like 'I won't take the case unless you pay me an additional 200 rubles,' then that's not right. The defendant may tell the prosecutor, particularly if he has lost, and the lawyer could get into trouble."

Then, Nina explained a little about the system, pointing out that at this time, all lawyers worked either for one of the large state enterprises or were part of a legal bureau, since no lawyer was able to be in private practice then. However, Nina told us this restriction was about to change in a few weeks, and a small number of lawyers would have their own practices, mainly those working with some of the new cooperatives, entrepreneurs, and joint ventures. But for the most part this bureau system would continue, three bureaus in every city, each with about five to seven lawyers, and most individuals desiring to hire a lawyer arrange it through the bureau. "If people are unemployed or are experiencing financial problems, they can still hire a lawyer," Nina told us, "because each lawyer must take a certain number of cases for people who cannot pay. The bar association will compensate him for his work."

Nina said that lawyers are normally assigned by these bureaus if the client has no one, though people can request a particular one, so lawyers do have an opportunity to acquire a reputation, increase their caseloads, or handle cases which involve higher fees. But now *glasnost* was creating as many changes in the legal system as anywhere else. "In a few months, lawyers and clients will be able to make their own agreement about the representation and about the fee, although the percentage to the bar and to the lawyer will remain the same."

Throughout our discussion, I kept thinking of the high fees

U.S. lawyers charge and the tremendous costs of our legal system in general. It made justice in the Soviet Union seem so much more financially reasonable and accessible to everyone.

I then learned that Soviet penalties for most common crimes are more lenient than ours, although the penalties for economic and political criminals are very tough. "A fifteen-year sentence is the longest we give," Nina explained, "and a person can get less time for good behavior. A person may go to a jail or a colony until his term expires or he is paroled, or he may be sentenced to what we call 'free obligatory work.' In this case he lives in a hostel and pays for his crime by working for the state. We do have capital punishment, although it is rarely used. It is reserved for the worst criminals, such as spies and (although primarily in the past) corrupt officials who have betrayed their trust and stolen vast sums from the state."

In fact, Nina observed, many of the less serious offenses, such as pickpocketing, stealing and hooliganism (essentially disturbing the peace) are considered misdemeanors and are handled by an administrative hearing, and a typical penalty might be a fine of ten to fifteen rubles or just a reprimand.

"Our goal is to make the punishment fit the crime, to have people understand the nature of their crime and rehabilitate them, so they can return to the community and won't commit a crime again. Also, when one person has hurt or stolen from another, we normally require him to reimburse the victim, and usually require a guilty person to pay for his trial as well, which costs about twelve rubles."

Yet while crime might be a growing problem, it was less serious than in the United States because, as Nina observed: "We find that people here are generally law abiding. As Dostoyevsky, Tolstoy, and our other writers have noted, the Russian character is very communal. We like community and tend to follow commands. Remember, we are born into a society that teaches that the individual's good is tied up with the good of the whole, so our culture is inclined to be more stable as a result. We have our problems, of course. We suffer drug problems, and, yes, we do have some gangs. But we don't normally have the more violent crimes or people who live a life of crime."

As she spoke, I suddenly realized how safe we all had felt on the streets, even wandering around very late at night. It was a welcome relief from the climate of increasing fear in the U.S.

However, while the penalties for common offenders might be less severe, prosecution itself meant almost certain conviction with little hope of appeal, although this was gradually changing to give the accused a greater opportunity to defend himself. As Nina explained, "A prosecutor, or more accurately the procurator, will usually proceed with a case because he has thoroughly investigated it and feels there is enough evidence for conviction. Because in my own experience over the last two or three years I've had only five acquittals, my focus as a defender has been finding ways to get a reduced sentence. I do this by presenting positive aspects to the person's character, or giving the judges a psychological perspective on his actions, or I show that he is truly remorseful, so he does not seem like such a bad person."

"Do you mean plea bargaining?" I asked, referring to the American practice where the prosecutor and defense attorney negotiate a guilty plea, usually to a lesser charge, so they can resolve the case more quickly and without a trial.

"No, not at all," Nina said emphatically. "We consider all behind-the-scenes deals to be corrupt. Everything I do is in open court. I simply appeal to the judges and to the prosecutor to be more sympathetic. Plea bargaining avoids a just punishment, and we try to be fair."

I explained that U.S. attorneys used pleas to cut down on the sheer volume of cases going to trial, and Nina pointed out that because their less serious cases were handled administratively, their system was not so overwhelmed as ours.

Then Nina explained how a typical case proceeded. "Say there's a report of theft at an office. The prosecutor is in charge of investigating the matter to determine if there's enough evidence to bring a case. If he feels there's not, he can drop it, or, if it's not that serious or a first-time offense, he can stop investigating and simply give the person a warning. If the person doesn't repeat the offense, then that's the end of it. But if he does, the file will show two offenses."

Additionally, the prosecutor might refer a case to be handled out of court, for example, to the place of employment if the defendant has stolen money from a co-worker in his office. Called "comradely courts," the guilty person's fate—usually just a reprimand and compensation for what was stolen—is decided by his fellow workers. "There is no criminal punishment in these cases," Nina commented, "but the negative side is, of course, that everyone at work knows. However, people do have choices about how their cases are heard; we like to respect privacy."

"Can anyone go to court to observe these proceedings?" I asked, pointing out that in the U.S. almost all courtrooms are open to the public.

"Yes, the courts are open here, too," Nina replied, "but few people are interested. We do not have the sensational trials you sometimes have. Usually only family and people directly involved with the case show up."

We briefly discussed scandals, and open court proceedings. Angela and I were curious about what steps were taken to punish corruption in the Soviet Union, and were informed that, as anywhere else, it depended on the situation. For example, if a court judge accepted a bribe, it would normally (at least in these times before *glasnost*) be kept from the press to protect the court system, although the judge would be punished, even more severely than the average citizen because he officially represents the state.

Still, journalists had more of a free hand in what they could write, and if a journalist is interested enough, he can get access to the necessary information for a story.

"In the last two or three years, journalists, like anyone else, have been able to attend court proceedings, and unlike the ordinary citizen, a journalist is allowed to look through the prosecutor's files. Additionally, he is free to write up any case, and we now allow journalists to take notes in court, something not allowed before."

A short time later we arrived at the court building, and Nina led us into one of the courtrooms. On a platform was a table with three chairs behind it, and in front of this was a table divided in two by a narrow bar.

"The judges sit up on the platform, and the lawyers sit on either side of the divided table," Nina explained. There was also a small wooden desk to the left for a secretary to take notes. In the center of the courtroom, opposite the judges' platform, was a podium which served as the witness stand, and behind this were several rows of seats for the audience. There was no place for a jury because it is up to the judges to decide a case.

"Our trials are essentially fact-finding processes in which the attorneys bring out all the facts, based primarily on statements by the defendant and all witnesses, in order to present them to the judges. We have three judges. One is a lawyer, elected for a two-and-a-half-year term, and the other two are lay assessors selected from their local workplace who serve for two weeks; their jobs are preserved while they serve. All three have an equal vote, but the two lay judges generally follow the lead of the regular judge."

Nina now quickly reviewed how suspects ended up coming to trial.

In typical cases a suspect is brought in by the police for questioning, and if there is enough proof against him he will be charged. This is called "detainment"; Soviets use the term "arrest" only for someone who is held after sentencing. It is usually at this point that the defense attorney enters the case.

Until recently, trial procedure was fairly standard: The prosecutor, who directs the case, investigated and presented the proofs against the accused to the judge, and if the judge agreed the evidence was strong, a hearing date was set. The defense attorney primarily attempted during the trial to get a reduced penalty. But *glasnost* was now affecting the procedural areas of the legal system.

"Now it's not so certain that the defendant will be found guilty, and the prosecutor has to work harder to prove his case. We're finding it easier to get reduced penalties, and there's a slightly greater chance for an acquittal. And there seem to be more appeals as well."

"Appeals? To whom?" I wondered. I had the impression that once the court had decided, that was it.

But no. As Nina indicated, it was possible to appeal to an appeals court within seven days of the decision if there were new facts or witnesses that could not have been presented before, and then usually the case would be reheard within one to three months.

"And then," Nina added, "if the appeals court renders an unfavorable verdict, there was one last hope—the defendant can made a personal appeal to some high-level official. Depending on where the trial has been held, he can appeal to either the chief or the prosecutor of the city court, of the Supreme Court of the Russian Federation, or of the Supreme Court of the U.S.S.R."

As these appeals were going on, the defendant might be kept in prison if he were charged with a serious offense. But otherwise he would generally remain free, though he would have to either stay in the area or inform the court if he moved.

Yet, while such appeals might be possible, in practice, Nina observed, "the verdicts are rarely reversed, so most people don't try these higher appeals, even with the changes."

It was quite different from the U.S., I thought, where one hears about endless appeals, and defendants frequently try to do so on the grounds of some technicality that could keep the case going for years.

Yet what about all these future changes? Might there be even more benefits for defendants, more opportunities to appeal?

Oddly, I thought, Nina didn't seem to like these coming changes, although because she was a defense attorney, I would have thought she would. "I feel people are starting to demand too much. As a defense attorney, I know I have done my best for them, and I try to explain why the result is fair. But the number of appeals has increased."

This emphasis on fairness surprised me. The Soviet justice system appeared not to be, after all, a heavy-handed, oppressive system with clanking prison doors in faraway gulags that I had imagined. Rather, in ordinary cases, it seemed that a balance was sought between punishing the wrong-doer, reimbursing or compensating the victim, rehabilitating and reintegrating the individual back into society, and making the defendant an example to others to preserve the social harmony. It was a very different philosophy from that of the U.S., where a trial could sometimes turn the seeking of justice into a win-lose game between the prosecution and the defense, while the media and news-hungry public might turn a battle into an entertainment event.

In fact, Nina was critical of some of the flaws in our system.

"In your system, it seems the criminals can easily escape," she said. "Your lawyers seek ways to set them free and may try to keep evidence from the court. But here it is not possible to do that. In court, anyone can be asked just about anything. Before the trial there has been a complete investigation, and we listen to what people in the community have to say about the defendant, even if it has nothing to do with the case, because it is important to know about his character. We search for the truth of what happened."

I reflected on Nina's comments and on our system's emphasis on protecting the rights of the individuals, sometimes at the cost of society's protection. Which was better? Our focus on individual rights or the Soviet's emphasis on protecting society and the state? I didn't know. It was certainly one of the more riveting questions of our time.

Now Nina asked us if we wanted to see this system in action by observing a trial. Of course we said we did.

We walked up two flights of stairs and saw a lineup of people, including two teenage boys, sitting on a bench. Several more people were standing beside it, witnesses and members of the family waiting for the trial to begin. Nina excused herself to see about getting permission to attend from the family and their lawyer. After a few hushed exchanges with them, she was back to tell us no. Although the trial was technically open to the public, Nina wanted to defer to the family's wishes. "They feel it is a private matter, and I want to honor their feelings and their lawyer's request," she said.

Since we couldn't sit in on the case, I asked Nina about the case I had observed in Baku, the capital of Azerbaijan, the year before when I had traveled to the Soviet Union as part of a legal studies trip. The case had been the most memorable highlight of the whole trip, and Nina told me that such a case might happen the same way here.

As I described the trial, it almost seemed as if it were happening now. On a hot, stuffy July day, our guide let us into a plain, boxy building that housed the First District People's Court of Baku. Fortunately, we had arrived during a break in the trial, and one of the lawyers working with the court led us in through the rear door to where the audience was seated. We squeezed into empty seats in the back two rows, and nearby in the rows around us several dozen people were packed together, many of them waving fans or pieces of paper back and forth because of the heat.

As we waited for the judges, lawyers, defendant and witnesses to assemble back in the court, the lawyer explained the case.

"A teenage boy is charged with an attempted murder. The problem started when he and his friends, also in their late teens, were playing sports at a local park. The boy took a pair of sunglasses from one of the players and they began to argue. A park caretaker heard them and ordered them to leave the park, so they agreed to meet behind some nearby buildings. There the boys began to fight, just with their fists at first. However, suddenly the defendant pulled out a file and stabbed the victim several times. Five of the wounds were quite serious, two of them potentially mortal. After the stabbing, the defendant dropped the weapon and ran.

"Then, the victim's friends dragged him to his feet, picked up the weapon, and flagged down a taxi to take him to the hospital. Because they were all friends, the victim and his friends decided to get rid of the weapon and not tell on the defendant. When they arrived at the hospital, they merely told the doctors and nurses an accident had occurred. But the medical personnel didn't believe them because the many wounds were too serious. So they called the authorities who decided to press charges."

"But why did they do that," I asked, "if the victim himself didn't want to press charges?" In the U.S., there commonly would be no case if the victim didn't want to press a claim.

"That doesn't matter," the lawyer said. "This was a brutal stabbing, and the victim might be afraid to bring charges. The defendant might repeat his actions. We do not know. So this matter is of concern to the state; we need to find out more about this incident. We want to know how the victim feels, and the attitude of his family, too."

Soon it was time for the trial to resume. The judge and the two lay assessors came in and took their places. The lawyers sat down at the table divided in the middle, and the defendant was led to his box to the right and sat down.

Finally, the first of a series of witnesses came in and stood in the witness box, one of the teenage boys who had been with the victim. The judge asked him a question, and he replied. The lawyer gave me a capsule summary:

"They are going over the facts and asking him what he remembers about that night. He says the defendant came up to the victim and said 'I like your sunglasses.' Then, when the victim wouldn't give them to him, they fought, and he struck him with the file."

The judge had more questions. He wanted to clarify where the file came from because this would affect his determination in the case. Did the defendant have it with him from the first?

Did the victim have it? Did the defendant take it from the victim? Did the defendant go off and get it during the fight? Or did it happen in the heat of passion? And why five wounds? And why did the boys try to conceal the incident? Then the prosecutor had some questions. After the witness answered, the judge turned to the defendant and asked if the witness's reply had been true, and if not, why not. Meanwhile, the defense attorney remained silent and jotted down a few notes.

As the lawyer later explained, this kind of informal back and forth questioning was designed to help the truth come out and was common at Soviet trials. While both the prosecuting and defense attorneys were free to ask questions of any witnesses and the defendant, it was usual for the judge to ask most of the questions.

Suddenly, the judge began speaking to the boy harshly, and the boy started yelling back.

"What's happening?" I asked.

"The boy is saying he didn't see the file," said the lawyer. "And the judge is saying, 'It's impossible you didn't see who had it. You were there.' But the boy still says he didn't see. Now the judge says, 'I do not believe you. No one will believe you. You are just trying to protect your friend. You must tell the truth.' "

However, the boy stepped down still claiming he hadn't seen it.

Next, the victim's father came to the stand. He spoke about how he went to the hospital and had been told by the doctors what had happened. At his urging, they called the police.

One of the people's assessors broke in. "Well, what do you think ought to be done with the defendant?" It was not really an appropriate question to be asked because it called for an opinion by a witness, and a potentially inflammatory one at that. But no one objected (the probable result in a U.S. trial), and the father answered, in a voice filled with emotion.

"I think the defendant should be done away with. He's no good to his family, to his republic, to the Soviet Union. If the defendant was my son, I would hang him myself."

At once a wave of emotion swept through the courtroom, followed by a palpable hush. Simultaneously, the defense attorney leapt to his feet, crying out his objections, and a grandmotherly looking woman in the front row stood up and protested. "He's saying such terrible things, what a bad boy he is. But he is a good boy. He has a wonderful character. He just made a mistake, and . . ." She attempted to list his virtues.

But the judge intervened. "No, stop. You are not the witness." Then, he admonished the father, woman, and defense attorney to all calm down, thanked the father for his comments, and asked him to step down.

Later, during the break, our group met with the judge, the lay assessors, and several of the prosecutors. We met in a large conference room where they had prepared an abundant feast for us. There was a big bowl of fruit on the table with apples, plums, and cherries; a box of chocolates; some small cakes; and several bottles of wine. The judge proposed a toast: "To our honored guests," and after some formal statements back and forth about how much we enjoyed being here and felt honored by their grand reception, we asked about the case. What did the judge think had actually happened?

"I think they were quarreling over the sunglasses, because the defendant had taken them from the victim and wouldn't give them back. Then the defendant's friend disappeared for a moment. I think he went to find a weapon, found the file, put it under his belt, and came back. Then, the defendant—the boy with the file—and the victim were fighting. The defendant grabbed the file, struck five times, got scared, and ran away. It's a horrible thing because they are all friends."

"What could happen to him?" I asked.

"According to the law, he could get up to ten years for correction because he's a minor. It would be up to fifteen if he was an adult. Since this is his first case of misbehavior, however, that will affect the decision."

"How?" I wondered.

"Because he won't go to jail if he's convicted as a minor. Instead, he'll go to an educational colony in this city where he can study and work." The judge pointed out that the boy's intention would be an important consideration in making the decision. If he intentionally wanted to hurt his friend or had planned the attack in advance it would be more serious. But if he just happened to hurt him in the heat of passion, the penalty would be less serious. That's why there was so much concern about how the defendant got the file.

For now, however, there were still a few more witnesses to hear, and the judge was not the only one to decide. It was up to him and the two lay assessors to come to a joint decision.

Yet though the lay assessors would express their opinion before the judge gave his, normally they would defer to him on the grounds that he knew the law. Moreover, even if they did vote to override him, the case would be reviewed by an appellate judge on appeal, and normally he would favor the view of the original judge. So in effect, the lay assessors were there more to make sure the judges were honest in handling their cases, rather than providing a real independent voice in deciding a trial.

The trial would last about one to two days, the usual time for a case of this sort, and the defendant's parents would pay for the trial if the boy was convicted.

So what was the verdict?

When we called later, the results still weren't in. But the lawyers at the courthouse were fairly certain he would be found guilty, since the prosecutor would not normally bring a case unless fairly certain of guilt. The only real question was what the punishment might be. "It probably will be ten years in an education camp," said one lawyer. "Though the boy has had no prior record, he has been well known to authorities as a 'bad' boy, and that will be an important factor in deciding his fate."

We had been talking a long time about criminal cases, since this was Nina's field, but what about civil cases? We asked Nina how common these were, and how much money people were likely to get.

"Oh, it's nothing like in your system," Nina observed. "Here we have far fewer civil cases and few lawyers. People get much less, and they can only sue for material, not moral or emotional, losses. And we have no payments for punitive damages either."

She made it clear that there was not much incentive to sue, because trials were long and expensive and payment to the wronged person was small.

If a person did sue despite all these obstacles, the typical civil suits usually involved accidents, injuries, and personal debts that weren't paid. In each case, the victim would sue the guilty person either on his own or through a lawyer. Then, if the victim won, after a trial which might go on for months, the guilty party would have to pay—for the cost of the trial and the lawyer, too. Beyond that, he would only pay for actual damages, but not the huge damage awards possible in the United States.

Nina explained why the damages might be so low. "Say a person is out of work because of an injury. The compensation might be just the cost of his wages. But since medical care is already free, there would be no compensation for that."

Yet, while the damages might be low, at least any payment seemed assured once a party's responsibility or guilt was determined, unlike in the U.S. where there is often great difficulty in collecting judgments.

"Well, here collecting is usually easy," Nina observed. "If an enterprise is at fault for an accident due to some faulty equipment, they would just pay. If an individual is responsible but doesn't pay voluntarily, the court would ask the enterprise to take it from his wages. Since most people work for state enterprises, it's easy to collect."

Then we asked about divorce in the Soviet Union. We had heard the rates were quite high, with about a third of all marriages ending in divorce, and forty to fifty percent in the big cities. Nina clarified that before legal proceedings for divorce begin, efforts are made by the local community and the court to bring about a reconciliation.

"We want to do all we can to preserve the family, but if they definitely want a divorce, they first apply to either the local administration or the court, depending on the situation. If both agree, and there is no debate over property and no child at home younger than eighteen, it's a relatively simple matter. They write an appeal, sign it, then give it to the body of the local administration that deals with the registry of marriages. An administrator breaks up the marriage according to their specific arrangements the two have worked out.

"If there are young children, or a settlement debate, then they must apply to the court and it will become a civil case. According to law, the court has the right to put aside the case and give the couple up to six months to work out a peaceful resolution. During this time period many couples decide to stay married. But if they can't work it out, the court will hear the case in which each party tries to prove his or her rights. A judge and two lay assessors will then dissolve the marriage and distribute the property."

According to Nina, it was very unusual for a divorce not to be granted, but in cases of long marriages of twenty or thirty years, the courts might refuse it if there is no serious cause. After six months, however, a couple can reapply.

It was time to go, and as we walked back to our bus, we asked Nina what she thought the U.S. and the Soviet Union could most learn from one another.

"I would say that you worship money too much and could benefit by acquiring more of our sense of community. It is true that we have material shortages and are less concerned about money because there is little to buy, but even if we had the opportunity to buy more, I would still prefer our strong emphasis on human relationships over consumerism. I think this contributes to our being a more solid, stable, and stronger society, and our laws are designed to help strengthen the community group.

"On the other hand, we like your competitive spirit that brings more life to the workplace and encourages people to work more. In the Soviet Union, where there are low wages and little to buy, people tend to slack off at work. There is little incentive to be very productive."

But then, as Nina observed, this relaxed situation in low-income jobs led to a situation in which many Soviets moonlight to pick up some extra money, though technically there were some restrictions on what they could do. "People are not supposed to earn more than fifty percent of what they earn on their regular job. But in fact, no one usually checks, and it's not a crime. Probably the worst outcome if someone is caught might be an administrative hearing and fine, so many risk it." In fact, Nina confided to us that she did some moonlighting, too, though not during office hours. "Sometimes I teach English, or I do some translating," she explained.

Now, as we arrived at our bus, Nina concluded on a note of optimism. She believed a more competitive spirit was being freed, and she welcomed this, though she felt the law itself would be slow to change, in part because lawyers themselves are set in their ways. "After all, lawyers have always been conservative," she observed. "When there's change, we have to learn new laws."

But for herself, Nina seemed to be ready to embrace a changing future. As we hugged our goodbyes, she commented: "Well, I'm sure we'll have lots to learn." Then, turning, she waved goodbye, and as she disappeared, walking briskly down the street, I thought about how the laws in the U.S.S.R. might change to reflect a changing society. Certainly, the law would be a place of major ferment in the years to come, as well as a facilitator of these major social changes.

CHAPTER 5

A Look at Soviet Education

While Angela and I discussed the legal system with Nina, the rest of our group were meeting with teachers and their students. Jennifer, as Scribe of the Day, kept detailed notes.

They visited one of the Soviet "special" schools, which offered in-depth training in particular areas of interest such as literature, history, math and physics, chemistry, biology, and foreign languages. This one was devoted to the study of English and was located in one of the new districts outside Leningrad in a low, white stucco building with a large open playing field out back. Although it was summer vacation, the students were eager to return to school in response to a phone call from their principal inviting them to meet some visiting Americans.

Our group was greeted by Vilna, one of the teachers, and led into a classroom where a table had been set with tea and cakes, a typical opener for Soviet meetings. Eight students were present, ranging in age from twelve to fourteen.

Since our group was brimming over with questions, Vilna began by explaining a little about the overall system. The Ministry of Education in Moscow sets the standard curriculum for all Soviet schools, even publishing national lesson plans and standardized textbooks. There are no local school boards or groups of parents determining curriculum. What happens in one classroom might easily happen in any other.

"All our education is free. Children attend ten grades, called forms, from ages seven to seventeen." She noted that some districts had added an extra form for six-year-olds called a zero-form, designed to stimulate the love of learning through lessons organized as games and contests.

"In the first three forms the children have four lessons a day, primarily studying the Russian language and mathematics. A few hours daily are devoted to fine art, singing and music appreciation, and physical training, and because learning about computers is so important now, we have started introducing them to first-formers in their math classes. In the higher forms, children go to school longer, have five or six lessons a day, and study such subjects as literature, history, geography, biology, physics, chemistry, foreign languages, and Soviet government and law.

"Lessons are conducted six days a week—students in the upper forms attending for about thirty hours, those in the four lowest forms about twenty-four hours—and students normally have about four hours of homework a day." As she spoke, a portrait of Soviet schools as contrasted with those in the U.S. began to emerge. Soviets place more emphasis on math and languages, and require more classroom time and homework. They embrace education in the arts much more and value an early awareness of world geography and political issues.

The educational system also provides for gifted students in the form of "special schools." Students could take preparatory classes to determine any special talents as early as age six, and if qualified, they could transfer to one of these schools. Here they were given an intensive study program in their particular field while continuing to fulfill the requirements of the national curriculum. However, competition was strong for getting into a special school, for in addition to passing a rigorous test to show proficiency, students had to possess a high degree of intelligence.

"Special schools are becoming more and more popular, and are based on our feeling that it is a good idea for a child to discover his vocation as early as possible," Vilna continued. "A child who shows an early interest in the arts, for example, can enjoy classes in music, singing, dancing, drawing, or sculpture early in life, and teachers can help children shape a direction toward a future vocation."

A great many special schools are devoted to the intensive study of a foreign language. While some of these students might become language teachers and interpreters, most planned to go on to a university and felt this skill would augment study in other fields, or they hoped for careers in foreign trade or diplomacy.

Students who attended regular school faced a choice after eighth grade. They could go to a vocational or technical school and continue their secondary school subjects while preparing for a specific trade, or they could continue with their regular education and afterward either take college entrance exams for one of the universities, go to a vocational school, or find a job.

"About sixty percent take the college exams," Vilna said, "but they are very hard. Only about one-third actually get in." I later learned from students studying for their exams in Kiev that the process was made even harder because they could take exams only for one school at a time and sometimes this meant waiting an extra year to take another exam if the student didn't get into the school of his choice.

Our group also learned that vocational and technical schools are the main source of the country's work force. Over 2.5 million students attend each year and are trained in over 1500 trades and professions. Generally these schools are associated with large industrial enterprises that provide the schools with tools and other equipment. Students have a chance to work at these enterprises, and when they do, they get a third of the proceeds.

All students receive benefits from the state while going to vocational schools and universities. These include small cash allowances, free meals, uniforms or work clothes, and lodging at a student hostel if away from home.

Other possibilities for receiving a vocational education are within industrial enterprises which have their own training centers, and about 40 million people each year, including students, are trained this way.

Summer vacation, from June 1 to September 1, is often a time for even more training and work. Many students go to camps in which, in addition to a program of recreation and sports, they might become part of a student agricultural or conservation team to clear fields or replant forests. The money earned for their work is usually spent on holiday travel after the camps.

After Vilna's brief overview, the teachers in our group had some questions for the students. As they replied, a composite picture emerged of a serious, committed, goal-oriented student who accepts authority and looks to teachers with respect.

The students did not complain about the long school week; rather, they seemed to accept this as the way things are. They spent much more time reading than American kids, mainly because they liked to read, but also because Soviet television was limited and generally serious, and did not greatly appeal to them.

Because Soviet students receive extensive instruction in geography—about two hours a week beginning in the fifth form—and are encouraged to learn as much as they can about other countries, these students are exceedingly aware of the world around them. They were quite familiar with many aspects of American culture, including authors such as Hemingway and Faulkner, films like *Rambo* and *Superman*, and the latest American music and rock stars. By contrast, it seems few American students know as much about Soviet culture or about the world as a whole.

In the U.S. teachers often complain about unruly students and the difficulty in getting young people to concentrate; there are drug problems and violence. In Soviet classrooms, there tends to be more order. Students listen, wait to be called on, and take it to heart when they receive criticism of any kind. A strong desire to do well, look good to their peers, and receive praise takes precedence. In America, students might look upon such conformity with derision, but here, both students and teachers seemed to like it this way. While the atmosphere might feel somewhat restrained or constrictive to us, to them it is calm and conducive to learning.

The students were remarkably similar to American students, however, when it came to free time. Sports are very popular, as is listening to music, socializing, and going to dances.

Because Soviet children are taught cooperation from an early age, with an emphasis on helping others rather than on individualism, students are particularly concerned about working for peace and helping their society as a whole. Some of these students had joined the peace walk to Moscow that summer, and others had attended peace camps sponsored by various groups, including the Soviet Peace Committee. In classrooms, children are encouraged to draw pictures about peace, and many volunteer to work for a day or two with conservation groups that spend weekends cleaning up the environment. As part of the required curriculum in the fifth through eighth forms, students devote six to twenty-four days during the summer planting seeds, pulling weeds, or bringing in the harvest on collective farms.

Students interested in the Party are initially prepared through extracurricular activities. At age seven, children become members of the Young Octobrists, which encourage small group learning and play through activities such as singing, drawing, looking at pictures, and having informal discussions. Normally a teenager from the Pioneers leads these meetings. At age nine or ten, most children join the Pioneers, a group that provides a mixture of political training, moral instruction, and social, cultural, and recreational activities. We would be seeing groups of Pioneers at St. Basil's in Moscow and again at Khatyn, the memorial to the millions of Soviets killed during World War II. It was interesting to consider whether all this might change as the Soviet system does.

The teachers also pointed out that in the ninth and tenth forms, students are required to take some training in military combat techniques and civil defense. Also, in these last two years of secondary school, they can apply to become members of Komsomal, the All-Union Leninist Communist Union of Youth. It's considered an achievement to belong, and about seventy percent of all eligible students apply. Membership is important for future Party membership, acceptance into institutions of higher education, and career advancement. Officials in the Communist Party participate in Komsomal activities, sometimes as speakers or as group discussion leaders. We wondered if all of this would come to change in time.

Just before it was time to go, Darla, Rowenna's daughter, took a bat, ball, and mitt out of her pack and asked the Soviet teenagers if they would like to learn to play baseball.

"We'd love to," one said.

"We know your baseball is so popular in America," said another with obvious delight.

Just then there was a loud thunder clap, and for a moment it looked like the game wouldn't happen. "It often pours in the afternoon in Leningrad," Vilna said.

Rowenna quickly explained the batter's box, pitcher's mound, and bases, and Darla threw a few pitches as each student took a turn at bat. Mike snapped away with his camera, and off in the distance the thunder rolled ominously. But it didn't rain.

Afterwards there was an exchange of gifts. Luci and Rowenna presented some children's books they had brought. In turn, Vilna had some children's books in Russian and some coloring books. The others had peace buttons with doves to give to the students, and then it was time to go.

"This has been a most memorable day," read the last line in Jennifer's journal. Yes, I thought, and just one of so many still ahead.

CHAPTER 6

The Younger Generation, Women, and Work in the Soviet Union

That evening, while other members of the group went to see the Georgian Folk Dancers, I went on my own to meet with the writer Viktor, and Rita, the editor of a newspaper for children, both of whom had met with our group earlier. A journalist from the United States would meet with us as well. When Viktor learned I was a writer, he had extended this invitation to me.

I was to meet him at the metro stop near Rita's house. Meeting at metros is quite common in the Soviet Union, where few people drive and directions to apartments are often very complicated. It presented me with quite a challenge—on my own for the first time amidst the hurrying crowds and fast trains. I clutched the paper bearing Rita's stop written in English lettering. Viktor had carefully sounded it out for me, and I gave thanks for my crash course in Russian as I scanned the stops swiftly passing. Still, there was the possibility of missing it, and I reflected how I never arrange meetings in public places at home for fear of missing the person and having no way to call. Now here I was doing exactly that—and in the U.S.S.R.!

The trip took about forty-five minutes. After taking the bus, I had to ride two different metro lines, using my metro map to indicate where to transfer. When I finally arrived at the stop I was five minutes late, and on the long escalator ride to the surface I thought of other things to worry about. Would Viktor be there? When he said he would meet me at the top of the metro, where did he mean? Outside the gate? On the street?

I felt very vulnerable, and the ordinary tourist program suddenly seemed attractive, safe and secure. I half-regretted not having gone to see the dancers. It seemed as if the possibility of missed connections had become a kind of metaphor for the trip—highlighting the loss of something known and sure against the opportunity for the new, the unexplored.

When I reached the top, to my relief, Viktor emerged from the crowd and waved. "I'm sorry to be a little delayed," he said. "A meeting that went a little longer than expected. Now we must meet the journalist."

A few minutes later Sally, the journalist, appeared at the top of the escalator. She had long blonde hair, wore a colorful dress, and seemed so at home that I felt for a moment we could have been back in California.

We followed Viktor out onto the main road, then walked briskly beside him through a crisscross of streets, past ornate stucco buildings where nobles had lived in czarist times. Now these buildings had been turned into offices and small apartments.

Finally, down a narrow side street, we came to Rita's, an older, four-story, pale yellow building with intricate white carvings around the windows. We ascended dark and narrow stairs to her top-floor apartment.

Rita reminded me of a spirited pixie. She hugged Viktor warmly and greeted him impishly in Russian, then led us all inside with an effervescent, high charge of energy. Her strong sense of style was reflected in her sleek black skirt and white ruffled, high-collar blouse with a scarf at the neck.

Rita's living room was large and luxurious by Soviet standards and as stylish as an apartment on New York's upper East Side. By the window were two large blue couches with fluffy white fur pillows. There were a few chairs with white powder-puff seats, several shelves of books in tall, dark wood bookcases, a piano, and a large twenty-five-inch color T.V. on a movable stand. The kitchen was fairly large, about ten by fifteen feet, and next to the refrigerator was a six-foot bed with a dark-blue spread.

Rita motioned for us to sit on the couch and went into the kitchen to get the tea and cakes she had prepared. Viktor volunteered to help her. She returned with a cart with two shelves full of pastries, including a cheese cake, white meringue cookies, chocolate napoleons, and pastry cones with thick, gooey white frosting. It looked as though she was expecting a party— not just the four of us.

As we seated ourselves around the dining room table the bottom shelf on the cart suddenly flipped over and the plate with the pastry cones crashed to the floor. Rita quickly scooped them up and retreated to the kitchen while Sally and I looked at each other, a little bewildered about what to do or say. Then Viktor appeared from the kitchen remarking, "When things like this happen we have a Russian proverb that calls it a sign of happiness."

As if nothing had happened, Rita returned and set out the remaining pastries, along with four cups of tea. I was secretly relieved about the loss of the pastry cones—with all this Russian hospitality I was already struggling to keep my weight down.

As Viktor translated, Rita began to talk about the writing she did for children and about her views on women and children in the Soviet Union. She had been writing and thinking about these topics for years, and as she spoke, as in our meeting with Olga and Ursula, I was surprised at how intently, dramatically, and with such explosiveness of feeling she expressed herself as she gazed first at me and then at Sally.

She showed us the publications for which she wrote, featuring articles for parents about children, stories and poems by children, and "how to" articles for children. "The publications are designed to cover just about everything of interest to young people," Rita said, "and also to encourage them to become productive, well-informed citizens."

Turning serious, she asked, "What are the biggest problems

you have with youth in the United States?"

"Probably drugs, discipline, and a lack of direction," Sally said.

Rita nodded. "Yes, we have some of those problems with the new generation. The children want to be freer these days; they have less respect for authority and many seem at loose ends—not sure where they are going. And as kids want more freedom from rules, parents want to keep control.

"But one of the biggest problem we have is that of loneliness. It's due to the loss of connection between parents and their kids." Rita explained that in the past, women spent much more time at home paying a lot of attention to the children, and the family unit was strong. But now that most women worked, children were on their own much of the time, and even with the close quarters in most Soviet homes, there was a lack of communication.

"Now the children go their own way; the parents go theirs. Problems and feelings of frustration result, and the children can end up in trouble." She cited examples of teenagers joining together in petty vandalism and noted how some had become drawn into the black market.

"We're not exactly sure what to do to resolve these conflicts or to alleviate the alienation in general that children often feel."

I mentioned the Soviet film *Scarecrow*, about an unattractive girl who so angered her schoolmates by her efforts to fit in that they eventually turned on her and tried to kill her, causing her mother to take her away from the village. Rita commented that in real life their actions would not be so severe, but there had been much praise for this film because the filmmaker was able to show the serious problem about the lack of support and connections children experience.

Rita pointed out that the problems facing children and parents today are particularly worrisome in a society where the family, motherhood, and children are considered its foundation.

"There is an old folk saying that says: 'The more children, the better off the family.' Many women, however, hesitate to have more than one or two children because living conditions are crowded, and more children can contribute to domestic problems if there is limited income or the parents feel tied down by responsibilities. Still, the state continues to encourage more children and stronger family units in various ways."

Rita went on to count the ways. The state had created more pre-school and childcare facilities, and with the addition of the zero-level form, children could start school earlier. The state had increased the amount of time for paid leave from work after having a child: A woman could now take up to a year and receive eighty percent of her wage, and the state was planning to extend paid leave to eighteen months. To add icing to the cake, mothers were additionally paid fifty rubles when a child is born.

Several other programs existed that encouraged women to have children. In some factories and farms, mothers with several children were allowed to work part-time. Some organizations gave mothers vouchers to stay at their summer facilities for free, and others covered the costs of sending children to summer camp. Additionally, some enterprises paid the rent for large families living in their housing facilities. Women usually retire at fifty-five, but if they have brought up five or more children, they can retire at fifty, even if they have worked less than the usual fifteen years at a company.

Awards are also given to the more prolific mothers. A "Mother-Heroine" medal is presented to women who have brought up ten or more children—currently comprising almost a half-million mothers in the Soviet Union. There is also a medal called the "Order of Maternal Glory and Maternity." When Rita asked if we had anything like this in the States, I shook my head and explained that too often, mothers with little education and few employment skills end up being supported by welfare and, if anything, are discouraged from having more children.

"Well, here we provide the education and the employment training," Rita responded, "so we don't have to worry about mothers with many children becoming burdens on the state. In fact, because we also provide child-care facilities, women are very much supported in being able to have both a family and a career."

The state also assists young couples and families just starting out, so that they don't have to put off having children. They are offered interest-free loans for building a house or buying a co-op apartment, and after their second or third child is born, the state annuls part of their debt. Additionally, a law legalizing self-employment and cooperative ventures, passed May 1, 1987, has helped couples to have families earlier by giving women a chance to work at home, allowing them to be with their young children. According to Rita, many women are taking advantage of this new opportunity.

Besides support for mothers, there are many programs for children as well. In addition to the clubs children could join at school in support of their hobbies—singing, dancing, model building, acting, drawing, and hiking—many public athletic facilities are designed just for children, such as stadiums, gyms, and swimming pools. There are close to 200 theaters for children, and in many, the children put on their own plays and musicals.

As in the U.S., there are entertaining educational T.V. programs, including a Sesame Street look-alike, puppet shows, children's theater and concerts, and the ever-popular cartoons. One particular favorite features a much put-upon wolf dressed like a steelworker, always chasing a spry little rabbit who presents him with one obstacle after another. Unlike the U.S., there is nothing resembling the programs which have been created from popular toy commercials, for Soviets don't make character toys and wouldn't create a program around them to advertise commercial goods. Instead, the emphasis is on reading. About one-third of all books published in the Soviet Union are children's books, and once a year there is a Children's Book Week where children can meet their favorite authors.

Rita took a few moments to describe the over 60,000 summer and winter vacation camps for kids, and elaborated on her own involvement in organizing a peace camp. She spoke of the Young Pioneer Clubs and Young Technician Centers in the country, as well as parks, sports programs, and amusement centers.

The Peace Camps are designed to make children more socially and politically aware as well as provide opportunities for sports, the arts, and other activities. Rita's camp was planned for 300 children aged seven to fourteen, and she wanted to invite twenty American students to join them. "All of their expenses would be paid once they arrived," she explained. "We would also like to see twenty Soviet children go to a U.S. camp. Afterward, all the children could write up brief descriptions of their experiences to be published in a book."

Yet there were paradoxes in their child-centered society. There is a very high rate of abortion. A reason is that most women either don't have access to or don't use modern birth control methods, and most men prefer not to use condoms. However, Soviets don't share the moral qualms many Americans have about abortion. Rather, it is an accepted way in which the overburdened Soviet woman with limited finances can better manage her life and assume the responsibilities for her existing family.

Rita also pointed out that the number of women desiring careers is steadily increasing—women are discovering their own potential, and are supported by the strong philosophical commitment to women's equality of Marxism and Leninism. However, although eighty-five percent of all women work or are in school, they suffer discrimination in the areas of pay and advancement, and tend to be concentrated in lower-paying fields such as teaching and medicine. While the fact that a large number of doctors are women—about seventy-five percent of the field—may appear to indicate women's achievement, doctors do not enjoy the high pay and status that they do in the U.S. The high status positions of plant managers and political officials that bring higher incomes and special perquisites such as the use of country dachas and access to *beryozkas* are filled mostly by men.

"Women today are experiencing some difficult passages," Rita said. "Overloaded with work both at home and in the office, they have little time for rest and recreation. Many women feel their husbands should do more housework, and more men are now helping out, with the advent of *glasnost*." I recalled observing many men wheeling baby carriages on the streets. "But others—especially older people and men—still think the husband's role is to work and support the family while the wife takes care of the house."

Rita shared her own story with us. She was married for several years, and as demands on her time grew along with her reputation as a journalist it created problems at home. Her husband was of the old school and expected her to continue to take care of the home and make his meals as she always had. "It was too much," Rita said. "I finally asked for a divorce. Now I am remarried, and my new husband is more understanding and helps with the cooking and cleaning. We give each other plenty of freedom; he often plans hiking trips on weekends so I can have quiet time to write."

While in the past a woman had few specialized services, now new enterprises are springing up to help her—delicatessens, laundries, repair shops. Yet Rita felt it wasn't enough. Women still have to cope with food shortages, long lines in small groceries, and numerous tasks that the average American woman doesn't have to bother about. Many feel that even the state arrangement for providing child care is not that helpful because of a shortage of facilities, which are often too full or too far away.

Since the pressures on Soviet woman are a factor contributing to the high rate of divorce, we asked Rita for her thoughts on this. "Well, divorce is something to think as seriously about as getting married. But if a woman wants her creativity and freedom, she may need to seek a divorce if her husband doesn't understand; she has to decide what is most important in her own life. I am so fortunate to have found a man who is understanding and generous, for it enables me to both have my life and to share it."

On that note, the conversation shifted to other topics, beginning with the role of journalists in Soviet society. We learned that apparently journalism is not a very high-status profession. "It's on the same level as teaching; we make about 150 rubles, or $250, a month. I have always felt free to say what I want in my articles about women and children, so *glasnost* hasn't changed much for me. But other journalists have experienced some significant changes in that they can now be more specific in their criticism of organizations and individuals."

I asked about the journalist who started the *Glasnost* magazine. He had been arrested and had his printing press smashed.

"That is different," Rita said. "He was not just criticizing, but calling for radical changes and protests. He demanded an end to communism and questioned the very system on which the Soviet state rests."

"It's fine to be critical of the bureaucracy, however," Viktor said. "Recently some articles have been published which criticize our ministers of water and energy. Our own history is no longer being hushed up anymore; we are now becoming aware of what happened under Stalin."

Viktor expressed his views on the bureaucracy, born of his work in the ecological movement. "We try to clean up our streams and rivers and change our technology in order to keep the waterways clean, but there is much bureaucratic resistance. *Glasnost* is helping to reveal many inefficiencies; however, since the old system has benefitted people in key positions, they naturally don't want to change. They feel they will lose privileges, so they resist Gorbachev's reforms."

Although Viktor thought the old guard was starting to shift its attitudes, he still felt change to be very slow and strangely circuitous. Because of a lack of consumer goods due to the lack of technological progress and modern equipment and methods, people could become skeptical again about the promises of *perestroika* if material results didn't occur soon. As Viktor put it, "People will work hard only if there are more goods available. Why work hard to make more money if there's nothing to buy?" Yet the system needed the support of the people to be more efficient. Both attitudes and systems needed to change.

Despite the uncertainties, Rita and Viktor were excited about the new opportunities to create cooperative businesses. Viktor was currently setting one up in music distribution, and his group was seeking to enter into joint ventures with the U.S. and other foreign countries. He asked if I would let companies in the U.S. know about his need for catalogs, general information, and such items as microphones, amplifiers, and tapes. He handed me his requests on a sheet of paper. "I hope you don't mind making the extra copies yourself," he smiled.

He told us an amusing story about the scarcity of copy machines. Some circulated publications were produced on manual typewriters with only carbon copies available. One time Viktor wrote an article that he was unable to copy, so he gave the original to an American friend who returned home, made twenty-five copies, and gave these to one of his friends departing for the Soviet Union, who returned them to Viktor two weeks later. "It may seem like a rather involved process," said Viktor, "but it's actually easier this way!"

In addition to the new entrepreneurs offering services, Viktor noted that many people were setting up small enterprises to make goods. Artists, craftspeople, jewelers, and dressmakers could now sell their own products, and some were now able to work at this full-time.

"I thought all people had to have full-time jobs here," I said, "and could only do this kind of work on the side."

"No," Viktor said. "Usually a person needs a state job to earn enough income, but there is a small percentage of people who manage to support themselves at a freelance profession. It's all right to be strictly a private worker, and more and more people are starting to do this."

He turned to Sally. "There are many journalists who make a living full-time by doing freelance writing for a number of publications."

Viktor reiterated that these new entrepreneurs could not hire others to work for them because at this time it was exploiting another person's labor if that person does not own part of the enterprise. We discussed the various sales techniques popular in the U.S.: making a profit by buying goods and then selling them at a higher price, paying salespeople commissions on their sales, or multilevel marketing where one person makes a commission from the sales of people under him. Viktor said these types of selling would never be allowed.

"If someone were to set up a pyramid structure here, he would probably be arrested. He would be making his millions by getting a percentage of someone else's work, and we currently consider that to be exploitation, which is a crime."

It was getting late, and Viktor and Rita each asked me favors. I was to inquire for Viktor if we could contribute any five-inch floppy discs to him and his friends. "We still do not have personal computers available to us; all of them are owned by institutions or high officials. However, more computers gradually are becoming available for schools and offices."

Rita asked us to mail a letter for her in the U.S. to a friend in California she wanted to visit. Permission to travel out of the country would require that her friend issue an invitation, in order that the government would know that the Soviet traveler would have a place to stay. "If I mail it here, it could take four to six weeks to arrive, or it could easily get lost. It's better to have personal contacts deliver our mail in foreign countries, when possible."

Sally agreed to take it since she would be returning home in three days. We said our goodbyes, promised to write, and started back to the metro escorted by Viktor.

On the way home I reflected on how openly we had talked. Before I had come to the Soviet Union, people had regaled me with stories of how repressed everyone was. They kidded me about looking for telephone taps and hidden bugs in hotel rooms and apartments, or being followed by the KGB.

Yet Viktor and Rita had spoken freely about their society and its problems, and I didn't sense any anxiety about being overheard or observed. Rather, the atmosphere was one of shared information and of friends assisting each other and opening new doors of communication. It seemed, despite the upheavals *glasnost* must invariably bring with it, its larger vision was indeed making for a more open, aware, and self-critical society, interested in thinking about new possibilities for the future.

CHAPTER 7

Peace Networking and
a Visit to the Baths

In the morning, while most of the group visited Peter the Great's Summer Palace at Petrodvorets and then took a hydrofoil ride along the Neva River, several of us met with Viktor and Irina, another of Betty's contacts, to discuss ways of working together for peace.

Like Viktor, Irina was active in a number of informal groups working on healthy alternatives, and like so many, she was empowered, independent, and full of ideas. They weren't dissidents, or "refusenicks"—the term often used to refer to Soviets criticizing their system. Rather, they were ordinary, thoughtful citizens who found bureaucracy constricting and sought ways to implement better ideas. We hoped our meeting would be stimulating for all of us.

Irina was fluent in English and began by pointing out the differences between their network and more established and officially recognized groups such as the Soviet Peace Committee or the U.S.S.R.-U.S.A. Friendship Society, which had branches all over the Soviet Union. I would later be meeting in Moscow with members of both groups, so I was curious to hear what she had to say.

"We have the same goals as these organizations in that we all want peace. However, because they are more associated with the bureaucracy, they are much more formal and will likely offer you only the current official position. You'll find that most people in these groups are members of the Party, particularly at the director level.

"Our group strives to reach ordinary people and encourages contacts on a more personal level. We feel that true peace will happen when people become friends, share their lives, do things together."

Irina's suggestion for a practical beginning was to have several of her friends who were currently working for improved U.S.-U.S.S.R. relations become "representatives" to groups of Americans working toward similar ends. Although they wouldn't have formal recognition from the Soviet government, these representatives could greet Americans arriving in Leningrad. The first project could be to create a center for future meetings.

"I know organizations which might provide facilities," she continued. "Americans who come to the Soviet Union would have a 'home'; everything would be open and local people could drop in; there would be workshops and meetings. It would be wonderful, don't you think? We could even start a small newspaper or magazine, and eventually set up centers in other cities."

Irina felt she and other group leaders needed management training since Soviets have relatively little background in this area. "We need to learn about making money, arranging loans, and dealing with business people."

She also envisioned making a film or video about these projects, for which their group would need technical and financial assistance. Betty suggested that perhaps her contacts in the U.S. could bring them films on peace-related topics, and Irina immediately thought of two ecology films she would like others to see: *If You Love This Planet* and *The Last Epidemic*.

"Down the road," she added, "we could put in a telex and a computer. But for now, we'll lay the foundation." She proposed the first step would be that a group from the U.S. should meet with leaders from their network of Soviet citizen diplomats during the winter, when it was not the peak tourist season.

Viktor suggested that we set it up as a Fam trip, which is a familiarization trip offered by some travel agencies or organizations to acquaint travel agents and promoters with an area. He then closed our meeting by saying, "I hope it will be soon."

That afternoon we embarked upon an adventure which proved to be one of the highlights of our stay in Leningrad: a visit to the baths. The baths made a major impression on me, probably the most lasting of any on the trip. First, they were an opportunity to see a side of Soviet culture most westerners never see, and secondly, the sheer physical impression was memorable. We began the process by meeting Irina and Viktor in the hotel lobby. We would have one and a half hours. Since the baths were segregated by sex, Irina would take the women in, and Viktor the men.

When we arrived at the baths, two more Soviets joined us, Vologard and Merla. Vologard was a strong man with sharp Slavic features, and his wife was also impressive at six feet—her heavyset build seemed to spill out of her flower-printed dress. If any woman was a symbol for the earthiness and warmth of "mother" Russia, it was Merla. After introductions, we were led into the old four-story building, up the stairs, then down a series of dark passageways until the men split off, leaving the women to follow Irina and Merla up two more flights of narrow steps to a closed door.

It was opened by a short woman in a white coat who motioned us inside. Rowenna had thought about taking pictures of the occasion, but she soon put her camera away. We had entered a large steamy locker room where a half-dozen women were walking around with either white towels wrapped around their torsos or nothing at all. There were several rows of benches and heavy, gray metal lockers on either side.

As we undressed, we put our clothing in lockers which had

no locks. Irina took our purses to the woman in charge of the baths. Thefts of any sort are rare in the Soviet Union, but, as Irina told us, "You don't want to give anyone the opportunity."

Then she led us into a small antechamber on the way to the sauna, where we sat in a semi-circle wrapped in towels while Irina explained the special procedures for taking a proper bath in the Soviet Union. We would do it the way the Soviets did, to get the most out of our experience.

"These baths are an ancient tradition," she began. "The Soviets have been using this procedure for thousands of years, and it is designed to stimulate the circulatory system and promote health. The first room we will be entering is the sauna. This is the first step. The heat is dry and your body should be dry as well so you feel this as pure, dry heat. We will be there about five minutes and it can get very hot, so if you feel faint, then go out. Second, we will go into the bath, which consists of the tub or shower, and after that you should dry yourself and return to the sauna."

It was apparent we would be going back and forth, between the steam room and the sauna, though in a particular sequence with some subtle additions. For example, in step four we would go back into the bath, and then would go in the steam room. For step six we would go back to the tub and then shower, have tea, and dry off. I felt it to be such a contrast with the casual American do-your-own-thing routine.

It was obvious Irina felt there was some sort of special, even mystical, basis for the procedure she was sharing with us. It had grown out of an ancient tradition, and Irina seemed to want us to understand and acknowledge this. This, in part, is what made the baths such an unforgettable experience for me, that we were stepping into another culture's ancient tradition.

As we stepped into the sauna, a carpet of heat engulfed us. "Watch your condition," Irina said. Seated on white towels with small caps or towels wrapped around our heads, we experienced the heat in silence. It felt as though we were being surrounded by a blanket of heavy, unseen webbing, locking us in. In the bin in front of us, the red edges of the black coals glowed, and when Irina tapped on them with a small brazier from time to time they tumbled about, exposing more glowing edges.

After a while I started to feel faint, and as if Irina could sense my condition, she cautioned us to go on to the bath if we were feeling too hot. I rushed out quickly, gulping the cool blast of air that hit me. It felt invigorating. The others drifted out, and Irina directed us to the baths.

We followed a narrow passageway leading through the locker room to the bath area, and as we pulled open the door, a damp, musty atmosphere greeted our nostrils. Rows of thin, shiny wooden benches extended from where we stood to the rear of this large room, perhaps one hundred feet by forty feet, and there were showers without curtains, metal pans resembling gold-digger sluice trays, and big silver buckets here and there. Women sloshed buckets of water over their backs or soaped themselves with sponges dipped into the metal pans. Irina pointed toward the middle of the room and said, "Now jump in the pool!"

Pool? I looked for something resembling the usual tile pool with turquoise green water. In the middle of the room was a large metal tub about fifteen feet high that looked like a beer vat. This was the pool. A metal ladder hung along its side, and a few women clambered up, disappearing on the other side. Irina urged us forward, and one by one we climbed the ladder and dropped in, savoring the cool, refreshing water that greeted us. Since there was enough room for two of us to lie prone, we took turns floating on the water.

Then it was on to the showers. Some of us experimented washing ourselves using the metal pans, and soon we were all laughing and frolicking like kids at summer camp—feeling the water whoosh over our backs, throwing it, squirting it. "I haven't done anything like this since I was a kid," said Jennifer, as we splattered around totally naked. A kind of camaraderie developed, a strong spirit of community I hadn't felt among the whole group before. At other events we had been more like separate observers, taking in the Soviet experience standing apart; but now we were totally a part of the event and of each other.

After another round of sauna, bath, and showers, we relaxed in the murky quiet of the steam room. Merla asked if anyone wanted to experience a Russian massage; she would also demonstrate the use of the birch branches that were bundled together and thrust into pans of water nearby. Betty promptly volunteered and laid down on one of the benches on her stomach.

Merla stood towering over her and began the demonstration. It looked like she stroked Betty gently all over her back and legs with her hands. Afterwards, she picked up a birch branch and slapped it lightly up and down Betty's shoulders and back. Meanwhile, Betty sighed slightly, as if in a content, blissed-out state.

"It will open up the pores," Irina commented to us. "It helps to get the blood circulating."

Split. Splat. Merla kept swishing the birch leaves back and forth across Betty's back, and finally, after she stopped, she put the cluster of leaves up to Betty's nose.

"Ummm, smells good," Betty said in a faraway, spacey voice.

Now Merla began the massage. Betty continued to lie there with the same blissful look, and Merla moved her hands up and down her back, legs, and arms with long, sweeping strokes. Then, switching to Betty's shoulders, Merla began to use small pushing and tugging strokes, as if she were kneading a piece of bread. Next, she moved her hands, shaped like fists now, with quick rapping motions up and down Betty's body. When Merla was done, Betty staggered up wordlessly, still a little spaced-out from the experience.

Angela took her place. I volunteered to be next, but right now there wasn't time—we had already been there long enough. After another dip in the tub, however, Merla would do it, and I eagerly looked forward to the experience. Once again we went in the tub, showered, experienced the water from the pans as it sloshed over us, or used the loofah.

Finally, Irina motioned for me to come with her and Merla back to the steam room. I could experience the massage right now. As I lay down, several people from the group straggled in and sat nearby to watch.

After observing Betty's experience, I had imagined gentle hands and soft, brushing strokes transporting me into a kind of blissful never-never land, and I stretched out on my stomach expecting this. And at first, this is what I felt as Merla brushed the birch branch across my back lightly as a whisk broom.

But then, all of a sudden I felt her heavy hands pounding me and then kneading into the small of my back and my shoulders. I wriggled a little, but the pounding continued even harder. I felt like her hands were gouging into my muscles and I screamed out: "Ouch. Ouch, that hurts."

But Merla just kept on. I wriggled some more, trying unsuccessfully to get away, feeling as if Merla's strong elbows and arms were holding me down in a vise-like grip. It was like being wrapped up in a straightjacket in a torture chamber, and jerking and struggling I called out, "Please, please stop."

From somewhere far away I could hear Irina's voice calling out: "Oh, but this is so healthy for you."

Healthy, I marveled. I could only feel the pain.

"She's releasing all the tension stored in your back and shoulders," Irina called out. "Just a little bit longer until the tension is released."

The tension released? It felt like Merla's pummeling was causing the tension, but my cries didn't seem to make any difference.

Finally it stopped. Merla flipped me over, and as I lay there limply in a kind of suspended state of shock, I felt her heavy form bend over me, and suddenly she planted a quick kiss on my lips. It was as if she was reassuring me that she hadn't been trying to hurt me but had only been trying to release the tension, or whatever it was, in a loving way. As if to echo this theme, I heard Irina's voice once again: "Oh, wasn't that wonderful? For the next few days you'll feel so good. You should do this regularly."

I nodded weakly. Then Merla finished up by gently slapping the birch leaves up and down my body, finally putting them next to my face. I smelled their piney, musky odor. So this was a Russian massage—it felt more like American rolfing, a kind of chiropractic deep tissue and muscle restructuring. Yet, while strong and demanding, this massage was also warm and loving—like the character of the Russian people themselves.

On the way home Angela commented on the communal feelings our experience at the baths had generated. "It felt spiritual, as if these women were mothers nurturing us, like going to an American Indian ceremony and sitting in a kiva, or sharing a peace pipe together. I felt so protected, so cared for, so safe."

We all nodded in understanding, and rode the rest of the way on the metro in silence.

PART III

VILNIUS
Tuning Into the Soul and Spirit of a Nation

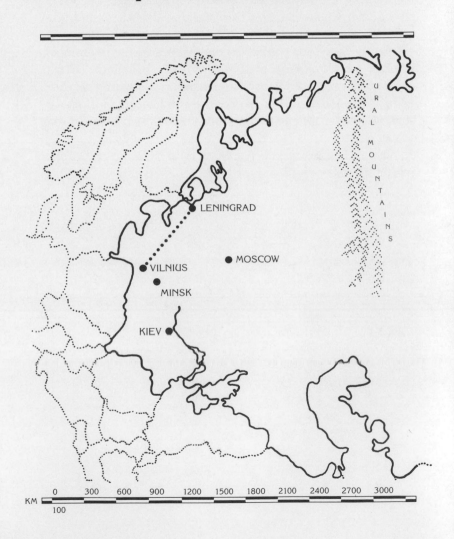

URAL MOUNTAINS

LENINGRAD

MOSCOW

VILNIUS

MINSK

KIEV

KM
0   300   600   900   1200   1500   1800   2100   2400   2700   3000
100

CHAPTER 8

Entrepreneurship, Religion, and a Visit to an Artist's Home

Our visit to Vilnius, the capital of Lithuania, lasted barely one day, yet in those brief moments the people we met gave us a glimpse into the soul and spirit of a nation. The nationalistic fervor and spiritual longing that characterize Lithuania touched us deeply and provided us with an experience we will long remember.

The flight itself was unique for those of us who had not yet flown point to point within the U.S.S.R. As foreigners, we received a special lounge to wait in and were allowed to pre-board. This protective Intourist treatment had two primary purposes: It provided a cushion for visitors unfamiliar with travel in the Soviet Union and helped to minimize any mingling between local citizens and foreigners—at one time of much more concern.

Our plane was an hour late, not so different from flying in the U.S. except perhaps that until the flight actually occurred, no one was certain when the plane would arrive or take off again. We passed the time watching the crowds of people hurry back and forth through the large, spacious terminal. When it was finally time to board, we would normally at this time have weighed our luggage and paid for anything in excess of forty-four pounds. However, on this particular day the scale was out of order, much to the relief of those of us still loaded down with gifts—and such things as typewriters.

Once inside the plane, I glanced around the cabin and noticed the differences from a western airline. This was definitely a no-frills flight with emphasis on the practical and functional. On either side of a narrow aisle were three seats squeezed close together without armrests or recline buttons. There were no slick in-flight magazines or earphones for movies, no microwaved dinners or elaborate safety demonstrations on video.

As we waited for the flight to begin, a strange misty fog suddenly began to rise from under the seats. It felt cool and refreshing, and Lena explained that its purpose was to freshen and air-condition. We all settled back. (The plane wasn't on fire as a few people in our group had at first thought!)

Without any announcements or blinking lights to remind us to fasten our seat belts, which everyone did automatically, we were soon on our way. During the flight two attendants served mineral water in small plastic cups; then we were on our own for the rest of the flight. No pampering or entertainment in the air, just straightforward flying.

Our morning began with a city tour despite our late night arrival. As our bus rattled along, we immediately felt a different spirit from that of Leningrad. We would later come to understand that Vilnius, with its strong Western European tradition, had a personality all its own within the Soviet Union.

The central plaza was surrounded by quaint narrow buildings with intricately carved molding, tiled roofs, and steeples. This older part of town looked much like an old European village. Mira, our Vilnius Intourist guide, explained that we were in a country that had ancient roots. Although Vilnius was founded in 1323, archaeologists had discovered ruins dating back to the eighth and ninth centuries, and the town is mentioned in Roman histories as far back as the first century A.D.

"The country was then inhabited by tribes who collected amber, and also were cattle breeders. Beginning in 1240, this land was organized as a state to fight the Crusaders." Mira pointed to a red brick medieval tower poking up out of the trees on a hill overlooking the square. "That tower is a symbol for us. It dates back to the founding of our town and was built to help us look for and ward off invaders."

This strong independent identity seemed to flourish here, as did the people's readiness to assert it. Lithuania had joined into a commonwealth with Poland from 1569 until 1795, when it was then placed under Russian rule. In 1918, while Lithuania was occupied by the Germans, the Lithuanians proclaimed an independent state for themselves, and in 1920 the Soviet Union signed a peace treaty with newly independent Lithuania. After German occupation during World War II, Soviet rule was re-established. Yet for all this, Lithuanians have always managed to retain their singular roots and independent ways.

Although the country is governed by a Supreme Soviet and Lithuanians study Russian in school, they still maintain their own language and customs. As we rode along narrow cobbled streets with row houses, Mira pointed out that most people preferred their own homes rather than the apartment living so prevalent in the rest of the Soviet Union, and the state encouraged this. Although numerous apartment buildings with flats had been built in the new districts, the state bank provides people with low-interest loans so they can build their own houses. They also desire to preserve the traditional look and feel of the city. "Anyone planning to build must have their design approved by the city's chief architect in order to get a permit," Mira explained. "The architect decides whether or not the proposed building fits in."

There is much entrepreneurship among the Lithuanian people, which has led to a higher standard of living here than in other parts of the Soviet Union. "Since people tend to work much harder here, they also make more money, and it is not uncommon for people to have both a state job and their own enterprise on the side. Common businesses include carpentry, sewing, and handicrafts."

The results were all around us. People, especially women, were stylishly dressed, evoking more of a feeling of the West; few wore the flower-patterned shirtwaist dresses typical of so many Soviet women. Because more people owned cars the streets were far more congested than in Leningrad. "Lithuania has the highest percentage of car ownership in the Soviet Union; thirty-three percent of the families own them," Mira said. "Many still take public transportation because it's often easier to get around, but more people are using cars, especially if they live in the new districts outside of town."

The abundance of churches, most of them Catholic, also sets Lithuania apart. People of all ages attend church regularly, in contrast to churches in other Soviet republics where we saw older women almost exclusively. Here we saw many families, younger women, and children. We happened to be visiting on a Sunday, and many of the children were taking their first communion. Girls walked in long white dresses carrying bouquets of flowers, and boys wore new suits and ties. Meanwhile, their proud parents strolled beside them or close behind.

Several people in our group found this to be an excellent opportunity to practice citizen diplomacy. Carolyn asked some of the children and their parents if she could take a Polaroid picture. As the image popped out and she handed it to them as a gift, they were deeply appreciative. Within minutes a small crowd had gathered. Gert, Angela, and Sarah engaged several people in conversation, with Gert translating: "We're from America . . . we just arrived today . . . your city and your churches are beautiful. . . ." The words and sentiments were simple, but they provided the basis for a heartfelt connection.

We visited some of the churches and had a chance to experience firsthand the profound depth of the people's faith. In one small upstairs chapel, several older women with scarves on their heads climbed up the stairs on their knees, lit candles, and prayed before a large icon of a saint. In a church, several rows of worshippers sang while priests stood in front giving blessings. All around them, gold-trimmed walls and icons glittered in the dazzling brilliance of hundreds of candles.

"They seem such a spiritual people," Angela said softly. "It's as if their souls are rising up to heaven with their voices." Our eyes were drawn up to the high columns and arches gleaming with gold and light, then disappearing into the darkness.

That afternoon, we had an opportunity to visit a sculptor and his family in their home.

Betty arranged for him to meet us at the hotel because we would never have found his home on our own. It was situated quite a distance from town on an unmarked, unpaved street. When Vanya walked into the lobby, no one had to point him out to us; he was the perfect embodiment of the artist with his trim white beard and ivory linen suit.

He offered to take as many of us as could fit in his small sedan, and it was decided that the artists in our group, Helga and Luci, would go with him. The rest of us flagged down two taxis, no easy task in a city with few tourists, and after Vanya gave our drivers directions, they sped off as if in a race to see who could get there first.

It made for a breathtaking ride as we weaved in and out of traffic, then raced out of town past several clusters of towering apartment buildings, the sure sign of government flats, then past scatterings of small, privately owned houses and cottages, many with their own fruit and vegetable gardens, which gave the area an old-world village look.

With a lurch, the driver turned onto a narrow road that quickly became a rutted country lane. We clattered along, occasionally passing even smaller dirt roads that veered off. There were no road signs and no numbers on the houses and we wondered how anyone could deliver the mail, but apparently the residents knew all the roads. As we came to a dead-end we noticed the cars behind us turning onto another road. Our driver looked crestfallen as he turned around to follow, having lost the race, and we finally pulled up beside a low white picket fence in front of Vanya's cottage. Covered with ivy and surrounded by two acres of lush green grass, fruit trees, and rambling vines, it looked like a picture-postcard image of an artist's house.

Vanya led us into the garden where a small gathering of friends and relatives were enjoying a repast of sliced cheese, cucumbers, small cakes, and tea. In moments, without any formal introductions, we were part of the party. Besides Vanya, there was his wife, Reyna, a married couple from Sweden and another from Germany, two male cousins, two women who were friends of the family, one of whom worked as a translator, a ten-year-old girl, and two six-year-old boys who chugged around the garden on bicycles while we talked.

Almost at once the conversation turned to the problems people experienced with the Soviet system and their concerns about whether *glasnost* would really work. Rima, the translator, who was in her early twenties, felt that the word was just a slogan. "Right now, at least here, we see only surface change and aren't sure *glasnost* will really happen. One reason is that the Party in Lithuania is much more Stalinist than are the leaders in Russia, so the regulations of the Soviet Union come down on us with a much heavier hand."

I expressed my surprise that, if this were the case, she could feel so free to talk about her feelings. She replied with a mixture of skepticism and hope, longing for the greater freedoms that were still in the future then.

"It is true we can talk more openly now. A few years ago you would never have been able to visit us. Yet we wonder, how long will these changes last? How far can they go? We still fear for the future.

"What many of us would really like is more democracy and local autonomy, but we're not sure how much we can openly talk about it or push for them. If people press too hard they might lose their jobs, and although our Constitution has laws to protect the person who speaks out, these are only on paper. In practice, people in power can do pretty much what they want."

Her friend Jena, a teacher in her mid-thirties, agreed. She had so many memories of repression, it was difficult to put these aside. Recently she had experienced this pressure again when her son went off for the two years of military service required of every eighteen-year-old male.

"He left last year and was assigned to a training camp in Belorussia. I felt it was unfair for him to be sent off to a place outside the country, and I know I worry about my son because his being sent away reminds me of the Stalin years when Lithuania lost so many people. I'd like to organize a protest or a petition to see if our young people could be stationed closer to home, but I don't know if circumstances are really as free as they appear."

"We feel the future will be shaped by those now in their teens," Rima explained, "and we are currently trying to lay some foundations. We have organized an informal network of people who support *perestroika*. There are about 100,000 of us now, and the group continues to grow. Our focus is on welcoming the changes and continuing to find new ways to promote them."

"Well, things certainly seem more open now than ever before," Jennifer commented.

"Yes," Rima said, "but will the government crack down in the future? Will things change back again? Our concern is deepened by the fact that so many people remain noncommittal. They simply stand on the sidelines waiting to see who will win the power struggle in order to know whether to support those currently in power or to start working for change themselves."

As we were talking, Darla, Rowenna's daughter, pulled up her chair beside ten-year-old Ani, who spoke a little English. "Would you like to learn how to make a peace bracelet?" When

Ani nodded, Darla pulled out a basket with gaily colored yarns and began showing Ani how to twist the yarn to create a swirl of colors. Then quietly, carefully, the two girls concentrated on making their bracelets. When they were finished, Darla gave one to Ani and one to Ani's mother.

"They're such natural citizen diplomats," Rowenna observed. "I think there is much we can learn from them."

Several of us walked around the group taking or posing for pictures, and I spoke briefly with the two cousins who were computer scientists.

"Our biggest problem is the lack of computer access," one of them told me. "Four of us have to use one computer at work. Although we can now own individual computers, they are still primarily available only in the workplace. This situation slows our progress and makes us restless for more growth and freedom."

These were the themes heard over and over in Lithuania— freedom, autonomy, democratization, and nationalism. (And in the next two years ahead, great strides would be made in these directions.)

As the sky began to turn gray and a cool wind whipped up, Helga passed around slides of her artwork and asked to see some of Reyna's artwork. Reyna worked at home as a children's book illustrator, and she now spread a large linen cloth on the grass and laid out her latest illustrations featuring her interpretation of such traditional myths and stories as *Pinocchio* and *The Three Bears*. As I gazed at her drawings I felt a strange, haunting sensation about them; the characters seemed distended and unusually thin with hollow cheeks, the colors dark or muted pastels. Her art conveyed the same underlying sense of longing, sadness, and pain about the human condition that I had sensed in our conversations that day.

However, there was not much time to ask about this because Vanya was urging us to gather up our things and come inside to see pictures of his students' and his own work in sculpture. He had set up several rows of folding chairs in his living room which had a cozy, cluttered feel about it—packed bookcases, numerous sculptures supported by pillars, paintings, several icons, and a piano piled high with sheet music. Once we were all assembled, Vanya turned off the lights and projected his slides onto a large screen.

First he showed his students' work consisting mostly of grandiose sculptures anchored in the earth, statements of strength and power. A simple, heavy grittiness characterized these pieces, featuring roughly hewn animal and human forms cast in bronze and concrete. Some were mythical figures, such as whimsical dragons and trolls, and many had elongated or distorted, twisted features.

Jennifer observed quietly to me that these works seemed to suggest life is hard, certainly not idealized. There was no way to interrupt the show and ask Vanya about such meanings because he was moving quickly from slide to slide and spoke very little English.

The next slides were of concrete bird-like forms, and I was again reminded of our earlier conversations about autonomy and freedom. These images seemed to want to fly, yet were held back in heavy, earthen forms. Finally Vanya showed us his own work, mostly blocky, mask-like faces and narrow, vertical bronze pieces that seemed to reach up to the sky.

At the end of our visit, since Vanya didn't have a phone to call a taxi, he and his friend Rima accompanied us to the bus stop at the end of the road. On the way we passed what looked like a warehouse, with a huge object in the front yard consisting of a series of balloon-shaped concrete forms perched on top of each other.

"Another artist lives there," Vanya explained. "He specializes in these large creations. We have many artists living here in our small colony."

We hurried to avoid the coming storm, and Rima boarded the bus with us, en route to an ecology meeting downtown. On the way she discussed some of the major local concerns. "We have a high rate of diseases seemingly induced by toxic chemicals. For example, we drink milk and then learn that half the cows are dying of leukemia."

I mentioned that we had similar problems with toxic wastes and pollution in the United States and that many people had sued the companies involved. "That's not possible here," Rima explained. "All our large companies are state companies and you can't sue the state."

One more reason why people wanted freedom, democracy, and independence.

CHAPTER 9

Nationalism, Politics, and a Meeting with a Psychologist

That night we met with Romas, a psychologist who taught management training seminars to various state businesses, and also had a special interest in investigating altered states of consciousness. Although we all expected to go somewhere quiet to talk, Romas immediately suggested that we go to the Baltic Song and Dance Festival. This was a big event: a concert of singers and dancers from the Baltic Republics of Latvia, Estonia, and Lithuania—an event which took place only once every three years. The people he had arranged for us to meet would be there, and afterwards we could go and talk. There was an economic benefit in accepting his invitation as well. If we were to buy tickets from Intourist for this event, they would be much more expensive than tickets purchased locally—five dollars as opposed to seventy-five cents.

The plan for the evening decided, Romas introduced his girlfriend, Gera, and as we waited in front of the hotel to hail a taxi, I asked Romas about his work on altered states of consciousness and presented him with a book on shamanism that I had written. At once he began talking about the high level of interest in shamanism in the Soviet Union.

"Psychologists here are very interested in exploring altered states because of our tradition of shamanism in Siberia. Shamans have long been the village wisemen and healers, and we feel there is much we can learn from them." He agreed to send me some material on Siberian shamans, which later arrived in Russian.

On the way to the festival, Romas talked about his work in the field of humanistic and transpersonal psychology, and it sounded very much like research taking place in the forefront of those same movements in the U.S., with which he was familiar.

"I do two types of work as a psychologist. I lead training groups for managers of large companies and also conduct encounter groups for lonely or single people seeking love. I have done some experimental work with altered states and psychedelic drugs; we tried to find out if these approaches might be useful as a stimulus for people to communicate more effectively in a group session and some of those methods seemed to help."

Romas described some programs which improve people's ability to communicate in conflict situations. One was designed to reduce the long-standing tension between managers of large enterprises and local Party committee members, who usually had different goals, values, and ideas about what can and should be accomplished.

"The typical manager of a medium-sized enterprise of about 2000-5000 workers is focused on the difficulties of managing people and motivating them to produce, while the local Party worker has an ideological goal to attain, perhaps a five-year plan. When he runs in a local election he may make claims based more on his projections, putting pressure on the manager to achieve what may be an unrealistic goal. If the manager raises an objection or doesn't fulfill the goal, conflict may well develop. We work on clarifying values, sharing expectations, and changing behavior, an approach we call social learning."

Some of the techniques Romas used included role playing, psychodrama, and reinforcement, helping people to become aware of their unconscious behavior, enabling them to change it into desired behavior. "We do a lot of visualization and meditation exercises, primarily to reduce stress."

By now we had arrived at the fairgrounds. We each pulled

out a ruble for the taxi, but Romas intervened to pay himself; and he did not let us pay for the festival either, saying we were his guests. This generosity was characteristic; the Soviets had limited income and resources compared with Americans, yet what they had they wanted to share.

Romas led us up a small embankment to the main path where we filed in with all the others on their way to the festival— families, young hand-holding couples, groups of friends—most of whom were dressed casually in slacks or jeans, T-shirts, and sweaters. The path opened up onto a large field with a huge amphitheater in the distance. Along either side of the field were small concessions selling ice cream, cakes, meat sandwiches, and assorted souvenirs. As we drew closer we saw thousands of people gathered, mostly sprawled on the grass as if at a huge picnic, and, off in the distance, groups of singers and dancers took turns performing under the fluted half-dome of the amphitheater, their rousing choruses filling the air. Now and then a few dancers passed by in traditional costumes looking as if they had just stepped out of the pages of a tourist brochure advertising the Baltic States.

We chose a small open area on the grass, spread out some newspapers, and sat down in the midst of the crowd. Toward the stage a group of about two hundred people were gathering. They formed a ragged line, with about a dozen of them holding up black, white, and blue, or yellow, green, and red flags.

We soon discovered that this was another historic occasion, born of this special summer opening the door to change.

"It's a political activity initiated by the 'Movement for Perestroika,' the first time in decades that people in this country have done something like this," Romas explained. "They feel encouraged to show their nationalism and desire for autonomy. Those are the flags of the three Baltic Republics, banned until this summer."

A sudden tremor of excitement swept through the crowd. People cheered and applauded as the flag-holders waved their flags. "Someone is giving a speech in favor of independence,"

Romas continued, "and the people are showing their support."

A line of police officers stood in front of the crowd, forming a barrier between the demonstrators and the stage.

"Is there any risk in demonstrating?" I asked him.

"No, I don't think so. The police are probably there just to keep order."

"What about the cameras?" Kurt asked, acknowledging the large cameras filming the event. "Is there any danger of repercussions for the people involved in this protest?"

Romas wasn't sure if the KGB or other authorities were keeping a watchful eye or not, but like so many others we met in Lithuania, he didn't seem overly concerned.

"I don't let such things bother me. The cameras are most likely filming the celebration for national television, and as for the KGB in general, I just go ahead with whatever I'm doing and I haven't been bothered so far. I am active in the ecology movement and in groups seeking political and economic autonomy, and I will keep on speaking up for change because I believe human rights have to come before everything else, even before psychological progress. Before we can change human consciousness, we need the freedom to express ourselves."

Suddenly Romas hailed a friend who apparently was looking for us. Gurgin, a tall, heavyset, bearded man in his thirties, was one of the leaders of an informal organization of psychologists and psychotherapists in Vilnius. He had been looking forward to meeting us.

Gurgin shared Romas's views on personal freedom, and he expounded upon this theme as necessary for the well-being of society as a whole.

"In order for us to have an economic revival, we need to be free and independent, and *glasnost* allows us to strive for this freedom. Many of us are taking advantage of the new openness—we see it as the first door of many that are starting to open now. Yet, freedom of expression, which you take for granted in the United States, is new to us. We are just beginning to develop democratic thinking, but it is a whole new mind-set—

people have to learn that democratic activity is perfectly natural."

Gurgin described the difficulties. In addition to the KGB members and political and economic bureaucrats who would lose their various interests and privileges due to the system changes of *perestroika*, there were also working class people in positions of struggling to survive. Many of them were finding it hard to know what to do with this new freedom, and Gurgin likened the situation to a poor person who is suddenly given a million dollars—he doesn't know how to spend his new riches.

It was sobering to be with people in the middle of a political revolution. Many weren't sure whether it was good for them or not, but others, like Gurgin and Romas, had the vision to see what real change meant and the necessity for having political institutions that assured people of their rights and encouraged freedom.

Gurgin continued, "The small percentage of us who are politically aware, are working in our little republic to increase understanding. We call on our history and the symbols of our national identity," he pointed to women dancers passing by in white peasant blouses and traditional long, striped skirts, "to help pave the way. First, the symbols and the slogans; then, gradually, people's consciousnesses will change, and finally their behavior. How can anyone stop the new vitality which has taken hold? Even if there were a reaction, an attempt to close the door, it could not last for long. Once the spirit has been inspired by freedom to regain its birthright, there can be no turning back."

———

Shortly before the concert ended, Romas suggested we leave to avoid the crush and move on to his girlfriend Gera's flat in downtown Vilnius. On the way he talked about the problems he had noticed in male-female relationships as a result of his research and workshops. Gera, who did not speak English well, walked quietly beside him as he spoke.

"I've been leading singles groups to address the problems of loneliness and poor communication, which I feel are at the root of our high divorce rate, as well as a reluctance for commitment. More and more people are putting off marriage because they are afraid to take that step; many do not feel ready for the responsibility of children."

"You could be talking about my hometown in the U.S.A.," Susan said. "What do you think are the reasons for this?"

"People aren't used to opening up and sharing with each other," Romas responded. "I find that men in particular feel a lack of connection with others. They believe they must appear solid and strong, and they put up a wall to hide their vulnerability, fearing that to show this fragile side may cause others to turn away or take advantage of them."

Romas believed that the growing independence of Soviet women contributed to this problem, as did conflicting ideas about roles. "Women today have high expectations of more independence within relationship and more opportunity to express themselves in their work, and expect more equal sharing in household tasks. But many men resist. They want women to continue to see home and family as their primary responsibility, even though they understand the economic reality that two incomes are generally essential to support a family above the poverty level. There is growing pressure to ease the dual burden that women bear, not only from women, but from many Soviet men and leaders as well, but in the meantime these different expectations create the seeds for conflict that help push men and women apart."

We asked Romas if people lived together before marriage. "Well, it's a little complicated because it isn't easy to find an apartment. Many younger adults still have to live with their parents or share an apartment. But when a couple is going together, roommates in a shared apartment may plan an evening out to give them some time alone."

We arrived at Gera's flat, and she led us into a cozy living room with a comfortable, overstuffed couch and several chairs situated around a long coffee table. She brought in tea, cakes, and cookies, and our conversation continued as if it had never been interrupted.

Betty talked about her Center's program of sending recovering alcoholics to work with Soviet alcoholics, mentioning that several Alcoholics Anonymous groups had now formed in Moscow and Leningrad, and she asked if Romas might be a contact. He was currently involved in all the projects he could handle, but promised to ask friends if they would be interested.

Angela wondered about women in management: Did Romas work with many women in his training programs?

"No, just a few. I work with managers in general, motivating them to be more productive and innovative. Because the economy is based not on profit but on achieving specific goals, there's been little incentive to produce more high-quality goods. Managers are under a lot of stress to fulfill a plan, dealing with workers who have their jobs for life, and I help them become aware of these pressures and learn to adjust or relax.

"Only about twenty percent of all managers are women, and generally they are not high ranking. Perhaps that will change in the future, but I don't see it changing now. Perhaps one reason is that women managers tend to have more trouble adjusting emotionally—they have to be tougher and more masculine at work, then go home to men who like to be dominant. It can create some real conflicts, and unfortunately, many women end up repressing their social or emotional life."

Because we were not scheduled to meet any doctors on our trip, and Romas was a psychologist, we asked him about AIDS in Lithuania, and the Soviet Union as a whole. He said that even though they had relatively few cases, people read about it sweeping through other countries and were growing panicky about the possibility of that happening here. As a result, laws had been passed which were quite severe. People who think they may have been exposed to AIDS are required to have a medical checkup and could be sent to jail for failing to do so. When a person knows he is infected, he is not supposed to engage in sexual activity with anyone. If he does, the penalty is the same as for syphilis—one to three years of hard labor, although a more lenient sentence was likely to be given. There was also a nationwide educational campaign similar to the campaign to reduce alcoholism.

The evening concluded with Romas telling us a little about his work researching altered states of consciousness. At one time he and his colleagues, who are psychopharmacologists, had investigated some of the psychedelic drugs to see if they might help people open to change without damaging the mind, but now he was moving in other directions. He had found that such drugs were not that effective, primarily because people had fears about the possible dangers and side effects. It was now illegal to do research with traditional psychedelics, and the new drugs posed a problem in that no one knew how they would ultimately affect the brain or the body. He was now researching for alternative techniques, such as music and breath control, to see how they could be used to induce altered states.

"That's why I'm so interested in modern shamanism. Shamans use drumming and controlled breathing to travel into other dimensions. Many people are discovering that shamanic techniques are important in healing, and I feel their knowledge could prove significant to human psychological and spiritual growth."

In the morning we had just enough time to see the marketplace in Vilnius before leaving for Minsk, the capital of Belorussia. (Belorussia means "White Russia.") At the market, farmers made extra money by selling produce they had grown beyond the state quota or on their private plots of land. In turn, those who came to buy welcomed the opportunity to select choice fresh fruits and vegetables.

We arrived as the market was opening. Farmers busily set

up long rows of metal tables—many of them in the open air, others under aluminum roofs—and carefully and proudly arranged piles of ripe strawberries, cherries, cucumbers, blueberries, and plums. Most of the vendors were older women, typical *babushkas* (the term for grandmothers used to refer to older women generally) dressed in flowered dresses, sweaters, or shawls, but there was also a sprinkling of old men and young people.

Some of us purchased some ripe strawberries and cherries for our bus ride while Carolyn went around engaging in citizen diplomacy with her Polaroid, snapping picture after picture of the farmers and several Gypsy families who had come to market. As before, people flocked around her in fascination and smiled with gratitude when she handed them their pictures.

Later, as we waited for our bus back at the hotel, Lara, who was with the Lithuania Peace Committee, arrived for a brief visit. A bundle of energy, she had traveled to several cities in the U.S. as part of a program designed to introduce Soviets to people from mainstream American communities, and now she wanted to greet our delegation as a gesture of friendship from the Peace Committee.

It was especially interesting to hear how her visit to the U.S. had transformed her perceptions about Americans. Prior to her trip, her impressions had been shaped by the press. "My friends and I thought everyone in the U.S. was either very rich or very poor, that gangs of criminals roamed the streets in most places, and that the majority of Americans ate only junk food. We also thought all the streets in America were very dirty as compared with ours, which are so clean."

We laughed as she spoke, comparing notes about Americans we knew, including many of us before our trip, who held similarly distorted views about Soviets. "Going and seeing for myself helped to correct these false impressions. I am helping my friends realize that aspects of life in America are much more similar to our own than they think. And, yes, some of the people in America thought that because I was from the U.S.S.R., I must be very special to be able to visit their country. Others expected me to be tough, unfriendly, cold, or always serious. So I was eager to show them the real me and that we are really not so different after all."

A few minutes later we began our four-hour bus ride to Minsk—a short distance from Vilnius, but worlds apart. The exuberant nationalism and energetic entrepreneurship we had encountered in Vilnius, combined with a kind of folksiness and nostalgia for the past and its traditions, created a style and spirit akin to that of Western Europe.

In Minsk, by contrast, we would find that acceptance, endurance, and quiet strength more characterized the people. The city itself, including the style in which the people dressed, would have a more heavy and somber look to it. Mira suggested this sobriety was due to the great suffering the people of Belorussia had experienced during the war. The tremendous devastation had forcefully shaped their modern consciousness, resulting in a strong desire to rebuild their city and look to the future.

"During World War II, the Belorussians suffered the most. When the Nazis came through Poland, Belorussia (bordered on the west by Poland) was the first area occupied; every third person in Belorussia perished, and Minsk was eighty percent destroyed. That's why you'll find it a very modern city."

Mira concluded her introductory comments by saying we would probably find the Belorussians more willing to accept authority; they were not actively seeking independence like the Lithuanians we had met. Interestingly, even the way the two regions farmed expressed their differences. The Lithuanian countryside, where many farmers owned their own farms, was dotted with small farms and quaint, distinctive little cottages set apart by wire and picket fences. But as we crossed the border into Belorussia, the fences and cottages were replaced by seemingly endless fields stretching into the distance. Almost all of the farms were owned by the state.

We stared out the window at these vast stretches of land for a long while, as if going on automatic pilot to absorb our experiences so far. Today was the Fourth of July, and I felt that we had reached some level of independence approximately halfway through our trip. We knew how to travel within cities and between republics; we understood the process of citizen diplomacy and had made valuable connections. We had grown in ways we had yet to fully realize, and we felt more relaxed— more at home.

That evening we went to the circus, and our Scribe of the Day recorded it in our journal: "Our evening was spectacular. All of us liked the small size of the circus building which allowed for a more intimate relationship to the show. We were entertained by a troupe of dogs, acrobats, performing seals, a contortionist, and a beautiful white dancing horse. We felt like kids again."

In the morning, we would wake up to Minsk—and to one of the most powerful and moving days not only of our trip, but of our lives.

PART IV

MINSK
Experiencing a Place Known for Its Strength and Endurance

CHAPTER 10

Loss and Renewal

My first impression of Minsk was of a busy city with low, heavy brick buildings, crowded sidewalks, and a jangle of cars, trolleys, buses, and trucks, moving relentlessly ahead on wide streets. There was a no-nonsense, modern-day feel to it. Our city tour was conducted by a pert young blonde named Shira, and it began with some basic facts about the city and country. Minsk had its beginnings in 1067 as a trade center between Greece and Russia; in 1919, Belorussia became a republic and joined the U.S.S.R. Now there were 30 million people, 1.5 million in Minsk, and about eighty percent of them were Belorussians. The rest comprised seventy different nationalities, with Russians, Ukrainians, and Poles in the majority.

In the bustling downtown area, it seemed that every square or monument was associated with past invasions or revolutions and emphasized suffering, struggle, or heroism. The city had been destroyed seven times by invaders and virtually leveled during World War II.

Passing a square near the railroad, Shira announced, "This square is associated with the 1905 revolution. The railroad workers gathered here to discuss their manifesto; fifty-two were shot and 300 wounded. Although they were not successful, we want to remember their efforts, which contributed to Belorussia's eventually becoming a republic in 1917."

Another square featured a large pillar in the center with an illustrated plaque on each of its four sides. "This represents what was needed to achieve success in the Revolution. The first plaque shows the October uprising; the next depicts the support of industry; the third, the cooperation of agriculture, and the last, the defense of the Motherland."

Shira showed a great deal of pride and love for her city and the people who had fought so hard to gain their freedom. We walked through Liberty Square, an expanse of land in the center of the city, and later along a shaded, tree-lined path to a monument dedicated to the poet Yanko Kupala. A larger-than-life figure, his imposing, twenty-foot statue was proudly draped in peasant tunic and cape, one hand held to his heart. Shira spoke with great reverence as she told how Kupala had helped the people to be literate in their own language and had written poems inspiring pride in themselves and their land. Standing in front of his statue, she recited one poem from memory titled "I Am a Peasant," penned in 1905 at the beginning of the struggle against the czar. The idea was that true nobility lay in the man who was close to the earth, and concluded with the lines: "Sure I am a peasant, a simple chap . . . but though a peasant, I am a man."

Shira pointed to a fern by his feet, which represented a special connection between the poet and the people for whom he spoke. A Russian legend was associated with this fern, and as we strolled through the park to a large fountain in the center, she told us the story.

"The legend dates back to the thirteenth century. Each year, on the day when the fern first bloomed, there was a big celebration and a ceremony of new growth and renewal. The young unmarried girls walked naked to the river carrying wreaths, then dropped them in the water to tell their fortunes. If the wreath floated down river to the right, the girl would marry a man from the right bank; if it went to the left, he would come from there. If the wreath floated ahead of the others, this was a sign that she would marry early, but if it sank, it meant no marriage, and the girl returned home in sadness.

"So, the fern represents hope for renewal and celebration, and it's at his feet to symbolize his search for the happiness of the Belorussian people."

This happiness has been long in coming. Because of Belorussia's history of wartime tragedy and a large representation of brave partisans and underground freedom fighters, Minsk was named a hero city in 1974. Shira talked a little about these heroes of the underground, their consciousness very much present in today's Minsk. We passed a statue dedicated to one of them, and she recounted his story.

"The man had disagreed with his father, who favored the Communists, and against his father's advice he joined the Nazi army. But when he witnessed the brutality of the Nazi soldiers as they invaded the Soviet Union, he saw he was wrong. He left in search of the Red Army, but couldn't get to them and joined the partisans instead. Since he was captured and killed by the Nazis along with most of the members of the underground, he probably would have been one more forgotten hero. But before he died he managed to smuggle out a letter to his parents saying that his father was right. We have a monument to his memory so that we don't forget."

Finally we came to Victory Square, a large, grassy field, with a tradition of bringing together the older and younger generations. "Each year the the great war heroes come here and everyone comes out to greet them. The children stand guard in front of the monument, symbolizing the joining of the generations in safeguarding the peace. This joining has a long tradition in the U.S.S.R., in that the young learn the stories of the elders. Teachers invite veterans to their classes to talk of the hardships of war and to urge the children to live in such a way that war is not repeated."

We learned that Soviet children are reared from the cradle with stories of not only heroism, but also of the terrors of war. They have heard about the sound of enemy planes overhead, their own homes going up in flames, death by freezing, being fed rats, pets, or living off boiled pieces of leather and even wallpaper. These memories are kept alive so that children will grow up with the need for peace etched in their psyches. When Soviets speak of wanting peace, this desire springs from a deeper source than we can ever realize.

Shira ended this phase of our tour by opening her book of poems by Yanko Kupala.

> "On the hillside the houses are standing like cripples.
> They cry, their war wounds on show . . .
>
> I'm happy to see Minsk is living and healthy,
> And healing the wounds where she bled.
> And out of the dust she is rising,
> And high she raises her head. . . .
>
> To a well-thought-out plan they're rebuilding our city.
> Though shortages still are not few.
> But nonetheless, surely and smoothly and yearly,
> The creative swing grows yet anew. . . .
>
> Our dear ancient Minsk, you are growing and blooming,
> Your squares and your gardens on view,
> With your columns and towers,
> You look ever more glorious,
> You are young, strong, and beautiful, too!"

As we drove away from downtown toward the newer parts of the city, everything looked so green, and Shira explained that a law had existed since the Revolution ensuring at least twelve meters of greenery per person. We also learned that Minsk is sometimes called the city of students because so many study there.

Shira then described how new planning was transforming the city, much as in other cities throughout the U.S.S.R. The planning committees work with five-year plans. Every five years, the plan for major construction is reviewed and altered as necessary, and we could see the results as we drove along.

A series of low, plain-looking buildings was followed by a complex of taller buildings embellished along the sides with attractive abstract patterns in colorful mosaic tiles. "The first buildings were constructed in the sixties and seventies; the style was much heavier because the emphasis was on simple functionalism. Now, in the buildings of the eighties, we're using colored bricks and panels to make them more aesthetically appealing. We're finding that warm or sky-blue colors help to cheer people up."

She then gave a detailed explanation of the cost of housing, true not only for Minsk, but for other cities in Belorussia and throughout the Soviet Union due to centralized planning and control.

"The cost of a flat is based on its size, thirteen kopeks per meter, and the average flat is about fifty-two square meters, or roughly 560 square feet. The flat generally has two bedrooms and a living room, and in figuring the size of the flat you don't count the bath, the kitchen, or the closets. So the average flat would cost about seven rubles, or twelve dollars a month. People also pay for gas and electricity, and perhaps a telephone."

This worked out to be around five percent of the average salary, which is about 200 rubles a month for one person, and 400 rubles for two, though the average family income often rises to 600 rubles because many people do extra work. These incomes however, are really much higher in purchasing power because of the many free services citizens receive from the state.

At the end of the tour, Shira read another poem that sang the praises of the Belorussian forests. Noting that Belorussia is sometimes called the "green republic," or the "blue-eyed republic" because there were so many lakes, she spoke of a mystical bond between the Belorussian people and their countryside. "It's hard to explain, but we feel a kind of longing, a spiritual tie to place, to motherland. Many of our poets write of it, but this sense of belonging has also inspired several of our best prose writers."

Shira also observed that when people all over the Soviet Union retreat to the countryside in summer, it's as if they are reestablishing their ties with the land and to each other. The children's camps provide plenty of time to play in the forests and sing and tell stories around the campfire, and many of the adults spend their month-long summer vacations traveling to seasides or to their country houses near woods, lakes, or mountains. When people were ill, they often went to resorts in the country provided by their trade unions.

I thought about attitudes in the U.S., where most people tend to think of land more in terms of property values or recreation rather than a spiritual tie. The irony here seemed to be that an American could own property, while in the Soviet Union, where people's bonding to the land went back thousands of years, all the land belonged to the state. The people might own just the house on it, though now new private property rights are being born in some areas. Yet then, as now, it seemed the Soviets' feelings of being connected to the land and regarding it as their mother were closer in spirit to the traditional Native Americans, who regard "owning" the land as something quite impossible. People live on it or share its bounty; but they do not own it.

CHAPTER 11

Khatyn

That afternoon we went to Khatyn, the memorial to the millions of people killed throughout Belorussia during World War II. On the way, Shira prepared us for the experience.

Belorussians were the first Soviets to meet the Germans, and because this happened at a time when the Soviet army was not ready, they experienced tremendous defeat. They were outnumbered two to one by the invaders, had no battle experience, and were armed with outdated weapons. In spite of the rising underground resistance movement and a heroic defense, the Germans killed 20 million Soviets, captured and deported to Germany another 3 million, and devastated the countryside.

"About a quarter of the population of the Soviet Union died. In Belorussia, 2.5 million out of 9 million were killed; hardly a family didn't lose someone. This monument is our memorial to them."

We walked in silence down the long road surrounded by open fields. As we approached the main grounds, there was a huge statue of a man holding the body of a young boy.

"Khatyn was once a village," Shira said quietly, "and this road was the main street. In 1943 the Nazis came to the village, took the people out of their homes, and burned the town. It was part of their plan of total destruction: Over 2900 villages were looted in Belorussia, and 500 more were completely destroyed. Most of these have now been rebuilt."

She told us the story of the statue, a symbol of the people's strength despite defeat. The largest barn in the village had stood here, and the Nazis made all the people go inside it. The oldest had to be carried in; the youngest girl was only three. They were locked in, and the barn was burned to the ground. Some broke down the doors and tried to escape, but the soldiers shot them with submachine guns. Then they set fire to all the houses.

Several hours after the soldiers left, one man was still alive; he had been covered by bodies. After working his way free, he started looking for other survivors. He found the bodies of his wife and children, took up the body of his best-loved son, and was found holding him in his arms when the Soviet troops arrived. The statue's inscription says, in essence: "The people remember; we love life. The people were devoured in flames, but that turned into strength."

Shira now led us into the monument, a vast open field spread with unmarked graves, headstones, and memorial markers. In the center an eternal flame burned, and near the entrance a small bell tolled every fifteen seconds.

As we passed row upon row of unmarked graves, one for each of the villages destroyed during the war, Gert suddenly broke into tears, remembering her relatives who had come from this area. "So many were killed and we can never know them. When I see this and think about the destruction still going on in the world, it really brings home to me the need for peace. Now I realize how much the Soviets want peace, too."

We passed the burned-out remains of a village house with only a bell tower left standing. "The bell tolls every thirty seconds in memory of those who once lived here," Shira said, "and the gates are never closed, waiting for the host to return."

She described the areas of unmarked graves, represented by square black stones, as cemeteries for villages. Fresh flowers lay on many of the graves. "During the war, over 600 villages were burned with their inhabitants, and nearly 200 villages were never restored. Each grave stands for the death of hundreds or thousands of people."

We passed a long cement wall with black inset plaques, which Shira called the "wall of sorrow," symbolic of the walls encircling concentration camps, and then came to a cluster of poles adorned with metal strips resembling leaves. This was a "tree of life," and it listed the 118 villages that had been restored at the time it was erected.

Finally, we paused for the traditional moment of silence in front of the eternal flame. Three birch trees grew along one side, and along the other side were strewn long-stemmed pink and red carnations.

"The flame commemorates those who died. The birch trees represent continuing life. The flowers show we remember."

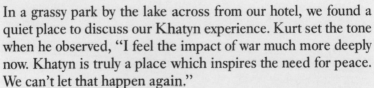

In a grassy park by the lake across from our hotel, we found a quiet place to discuss our Khatyn experience. Kurt set the tone when he observed, "I feel the impact of war much more deeply now. Khatyn is truly a place which inspires the need for peace. We can't let that happen again."

Mike felt overwhelmed by the tremendous power of the memorial. "The rebuilding they have done is phenomenal; so much was destroyed, yet they found the will to go on. The statue clearly shows how the human spirit survives, endures, and makes anything possible."

At that moment Gert and Sarah arrived with a Soviet couple they had met in the hotel the night before. Andre and Anna, both in their twenties, worked as computer programmers. The four met when Andre overheard Gert speaking fluent Russian, engaged her in conversation, and within minutes, a sudden and strong sense of kinship developed because Gert's relatives had lived in Minsk.

Betty invited them to find a place in the circle and explained what we were doing. We were happy to have the Soviets join us, and we asked them about the Khatyn monument.

As Gert translated, Andre slowly and thoughtfully replied. "We feel it's important to remember the soul and spirit of the people who died so that those who come after them will understand that we must have peace. There has been enough suffering. We are proud of the progress we have made in rebuilding, in exploring new frontiers in space, in conquering illiteracy, in educating our people. We wish to continue to look to the future with a renewed sense of hope."

As it turned out, Andre and Anna were extremely open-minded people and as curious about us as we were about them. "What do Americans really think of Soviets?" Anna wanted to know, and we dove into as many key controversial areas as we could in our short time together. It was exciting and evocative to discuss such issues as the arms race and whether we could really trust each other in the days ahead. We concluded that much of the mutual hostility was due to outdated thinking, special interests that didn't focus on the welfare of people, and the needs of *both* sides to feel safe from aggression. We acknowledged the irony of each side wanting peace yet preparing for defense, and we asked Andre for his views on how best to work for peace.

"I am an ordinary citizen and can only give you my own ideas," he replied. "But I think I speak for many of my friends as well when I say we need more relationships with each other, more *glasnost*. Before, when things were closed, we were afraid of each other, but as we meet face to face as we are doing now, and see there is nothing to fear, then we can begin working together to destroy all arms and get on with the process of living."

We all shared our ideas for peace. Bill felt that sending telegrams and writing letters to pressure our leaders was imperative. "Our former President Eisenhower said that peace will come when the people demand it."

Andre expressed the need for more volunteer peace groups and peace-oriented activities, such as the Peace Walk, which was currently progressing from Leningrad to Moscow, or peace funds to which people could contribute. These funds might even be used to provide housing or other basic needs, so that the poorer segments of society could begin to experience some relief.

Later, I went for a walk along the lake. It was a placid scene that might have been plucked from a Russian country village, yet it was just across the busy main street in front of our hotel. Four boys in bathing suits were swimming near a trail on the other side, and as the sky darkened into night they gathered around a small log fire. I decided to speak to one of the fishermen poised at the water's edge. He knew enough English to tell me he came here each night to fish and that he lived in an apartment on the other side of the lake. We said goodnight and I walked on, feeling some frustration at the language barrier. There was so much I wanted to say.

A silver moon glimmered in the sky, casting its reflection on the rippling water. A feeling of exhilaration came over me — I felt completely safe and free. The faces of the people I passed seemed friendly and inviting, such a different picture from the view I once had of the Soviet Union. Now, here I was wandering securely in the middle of a wooded park with the sparkle of the moon overhead. It struck me as a fitting image for our peace-filled day, and as I turned to head back, it seemed to follow me home.

PART V

MOSCOW
The Center

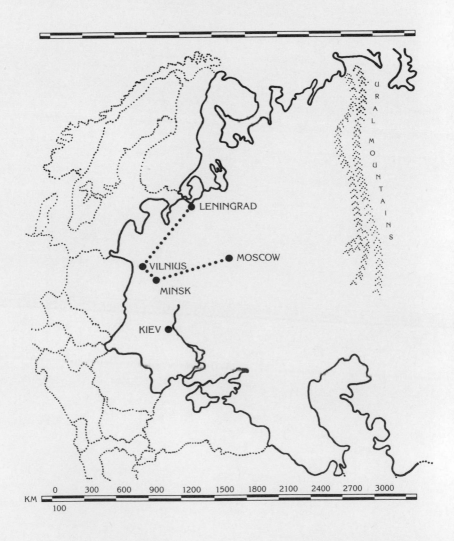

CHAPTER 12

A Tour of Moscow, Finding a Place to Live, and a Conversation with a Black Marketeer

When we arrived in Moscow the next afternoon, our Intourist guide was waiting at the airport. Zoya was a short, stocky woman of about fifty, with an animated personality. As soon as she saw us she zoomed over, helped us with our baggage, then whisked us off by bus to the Cosmos Hotel at the other end of the city.

On the way, we received a capsule summary of Moscow and also learned a little about Zoya. She had worked for Intourist nearly twenty-five years, was married to a journalist, and had several children and grandchildren. She told us that the traffic was heavier than was usual at the end of the working day, but I observed it was nothing like traffic in the larger U.S. cities. "We want to keep our environment pollution free, and make it easier for people to get around," Zoya said. "That's why few people own cars, and, besides, having a car is very expensive."

We were still in the outlying districts, characterized by identical-looking, plain white apartment buildings, which Zoya explained were built for efficiency. "Although Moscow is over 800 years old, eighty percent of it has been built since World War II. It keeps expanding into these newer residential districts, all of which are linked by the metro. The buildings we are now passing were built in the sixties."

As we neared the central city, the buildings were older: "Here the houses were built mostly in the fifties . . . Now we're passing the bridge over the railroad that was the boundary of the city until 1940 . . . There on your left you'll see some of the palaces built for the nobility at the end of the eighteenth century." I felt as if I was in a time capsule going backwards, that would go forward again as we rode to the opposite end of the city.

Zoya continued her capsule portrait of the city, hopping from one fact to another. Moscow became the capital of the Soviet Union once again after the Bolshevik Revolution in 1918. In 1711, Peter the Great moved the capital from Moscow to St. Petersburg. Then Lenin restored it to Moscow as a symbol of revolution and to protect the government seat from foreign invasion. As we passed the state university, Zoya spoke of the importance their country places on higher education. "We have over eighty higher learning institutions here and well over a half-million students. Additionally, our Academy of Science has 400 scientific research centers."

As we passed several theaters and stadiums downtown, Zoya delivered some more impressive statistics. "There are over 500 permanent theaters in Moscow, 150 of them for children. We have thirty ballet companies, thirty opera houses, and our Moscow Film Company makes close to seventy films a year. The Lenin library has over thirty million books comprising all 278 languages of the U.S.S.R., and our Olympic stadium holds 45,000 people. Seventy-six public swimming pools operate year-round."

Perhaps most interesting were the bits and pieces of ancient legends she told us. Like most Soviet visitors, we thought Red Square got its name from the Communist Revolution. But Zoya explained that "red" in ancient Russian means "beautiful," and it was named the Red, or beautiful, Square in the seventeenth century.

She then told the fascinating, though grisly, legend of St. Basil's Cathedral. It was built in the sixteenth century during the reign of Ivan the Terrible, who ruled from 1547 to 1584. After he captured the city of Kazan and ousted the Mongols in

1552, the church was later built (between 1561 and 1565) as a monument to show that this was a victory for all the people. According to legend, when the church was finished Ivan asked the architect if he could build anything else as beautiful, and when he said yes, Ivan blinded him to prevent that from ever happening.

"Is that really true?" Angela asked.

"We don't know. It's a legend," Zoya replied. We then passed her downtown apartment building, and she told us about housing in Moscow. "We have two bedrooms, a living room, kitchen, and a balcony with a small garden for three people— my husband, myself, and our daughter. Our apartment is quite typical."

Moscow, like Leningrad, Zoya explained, has no private homes because there are so many people; apparently there is room only for apartments and flats, most of which are government owned and regulated.

"The government tries to match the size of the apartment to the size of the family. Currently the standard amount of housing space is twelve square meters per person. However, if someone needs more room for their work, as in the case of a scientist, writer, composer, or artist, it is possible to get more."

To secure an apartment, Zoya tells us, people would go to the housing commission in the area where they want to live, applying either to the housing commission, which is part of the Council of People's Deputies in the city, or to the housing commission of a local trade union or enterprise. The applications are reviewed and decisions on who gets first priority is based on need. For example, if a family is living in a crowded situation of less than five square meters per person, they will usually get first priority.

Another housing option is to own a cooperative apartment, which numbers about twenty percent of all available apartments. Some people choose cooperatives because they don't want to wait for a government apartment, or they like the idea of owning rather than paying rent. "It's more expensive," Zoya said, "but it's possible to get a loan from the government at a low interest rate. These apartments cost anywhere from 5,000 to 10,000 rubles. Normally, people pay thirty or forty percent down, and sometimes their trade union pays a portion of this; they can get the rest as a loan from the government at five percent interest over fifteen to twenty years. After the final payment they own the apartment, but it can be sold back only to the co-op, and only for the same price."

Zoya pointed out that there were several options available in preparing for cooperative ownership. In addition to simply saving money, taking on extra work, or going to the Far East or the North for a few years in order to considerably increase one's earning power, some families chose to join a construction team. A husband and/or wife would receive a short course on construction under the direction of a skilled building expert, then assist in building one or several apartment buildings and perhaps other facilities associated with the complex as well, such as cafes, daycare centers, or schools. While they work on the construction, which generally takes about a year, their regular jobs are held for them. The government covers all the expenses for building. After the project is finished, the young family has contributed both to housing for others and now has a place to live.

Another method of ownership Zoya spoke of is for people to pool their money and build an apartment complex on their own, partly because they don't want to wait for state-provided housing. This arrangement is also attractive because they can create more living space than is normally available in government apartments. Most people, however, live in government apartments because it is less expensive.

We now headed for our hotel, the Cosmos, which looked much like the Pribaltiskaya in Leningrad. It had close to three thousand rooms and stood at the top of a small rise, resembling a modern fortress of steel and concrete, showing a sheer, semicircular face with multiple rows of equally spaced windows and columns.

The Cosmos, which literally means "space," was built to acknowledge Soviet achievements in space, as were many of the attractions surrounding it. Zoya pointed across the street to a thin, curving tower that looked like a bent needle. "That monument commemorates our cosmonauts, and it is made of titanium, the same material used in building space vehicles."

There were abundant points of interest associated with peace and international understanding. The main street was Prospect Mira (meaning "Peace Avenue"), so named when the International Symposium of Democratic Youth of the World stayed here and conducted a peace march for their opening ceremony. Off in the distance was an exhibit park devoted to Soviet economic achievements emphasizing the importance of peace to a prospering economy.

The first place everyone wanted to visit was Red Square, the heart of the Soviet Union and the home of the Kremlin and St. Basil's Cathedral. The plan was to relax after a day of traveling, then go by the metro after supper.

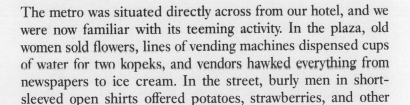

The metro was situated directly across from our hotel, and we were now familiar with its teeming activity. In the plaza, old women sold flowers, lines of vending machines dispensed cups of water for two kopeks, and vendors hawked everything from newspapers to ice cream. In the street, burly men in short-sleeved open shirts offered potatoes, strawberries, and other produce from the backs of trucks.

Mike and I snapped a few pictures as we raced after Betty and the group, and in moments we were through the gates and speeding down the escalator to the train platform below. The pace was faster, the crowd larger, and the press of bodies closer than in Leningrad. I heard Betty's voice from what seemed like very far away, though she was only on the opposite side of the car.

"Try to get off when I do. If you become separated, just get off at the next stop and wait there—we'll come for you."

For a moment I felt like a little kid about to lose my parent, but then the car lurched to a halt and there was no more time to think. At once there was a surge to the door and I was propelled out with the crowd. Several of us tried to push our way back in when we heard Betty yell, "No, not here; it's not our stop."

As I struggled against the tide, I imagined myself a salmon trying to swim upstream. Mercifully, after the people exiting were finally off, the current surged the other way. Success! Just as I managed to get back on the car, the doors snapped shut with a loud whap and we took off. I felt my feet slide out and grabbed around for someone or something to hold onto, but there was nowhere to fall. We were packed in like sardines.

"The next stop is ours," Betty cried out, and this time I prepared myself for the launch onto the platform, where we stopped briefly to make sure we were all there.

"Is it always like this?" I asked Betty.

"Just be glad this isn't rush hour," she replied. She led us down a long dark corridor and through a tunnel that opened into a sparkling white marble room. It felt as though we had emerged from the bowels of the earth into the light and into an underground palace. We admired the graceful marble columns with gold fluted tips resembling flowers and the bronze plaques with Russian lettering adorning the walls. The place seemed like a museum, but this was actually just a typical station on a special line of the Moscow metro.

"It's called the Ring Line," Betty explained, "and it encircles the city. All the stations are this beautiful."

As we walked up and down the platform in a kind of awed reverence, we were oblivious to the crowds streaming by. It was like a shrine dedicated to the transporting of people, and even with thousands passing through, there wasn't one scrap of paper or one mark of the graffiti artist.

Several blocks later we arrived at Red Square, agreeing to

meet back at the metro within an hour in case anyone became separated from the group. Red Square was more of an elongated plaza, and since it was 8:00 P.M. only a few people strolled about, allowing us to more fully appreciate its magnificence. There before us were the high stern walls of the Kremlin. Completing the other three sides of the square were the whimsical, multicolored onion domes of St. Basil's Cathedral, the stately towers of the Russian historical museum, and the intricate, fluted columns of the Soviet Union's largest department store, the Gum.

A small crowd of people clustered around Lenin's tomb, a large black marble monument with the word LENIN on top in bold Russian letters. When we moved in behind the crowd, we were told they were waiting to see the changing of the guard which occurred each hour on the hour. So we waited. Precisely at 9:00 P.M., the bell in the Kremlin tower gonged and the three guards by the tomb goose-stepped towards the far Kremlin gate as three Kremlin guards marched towards the tomb with faces as impassive and stiff as the rifles they carried. When it was over, the crowd quickly dispersed and we continued on to the Kremlin gate.

Most of the time the guards allowed people to wander here and there; groups of teenagers sat casually on the sidewalk. But whenever a black limousine carrying government officials went in or out, a different scenario ensued. Before the car appeared, a light at the Kremlin gate changed from red to green, a policeman blew his whistle, and everyone near the gate cleared the square to let the car pass. Each time this happened a buzz spread through the crowd as onlookers wondered who the privileged Party member in the car might be. It was like seeing the Soviet version of royalty come and go, people properly showing their respect by lining up to watch, and I imagined the subjects of a former time honoring their czar as he rode by in his coach.

A few artists were finishing sketches of the Kremlin or St. Basil's and seemed oblivious to us as we stopped to watch or take pictures. I pointed my camera up to the domes of St. Basil's to capture a particularly intriguing cloud formation, and afterward I looked around to discover that the rest of the group had vanished. I glanced across the square, then searched briefly down a few side streets. Where did they go? Since it was almost time to meet back at the metro, I headed toward the station and that's where I met the black marketeer.

As I was changing my camera lens a neatly dressed young man in his twenties approached me, accompanied by two friends. He carried a black satchel over his shoulder.

"That's a nice camera. Do you take many pictures?"

"Yes," I said, struggling with the lens. I hadn't been looking for a conversation and was obviously distracted, but he persisted.

"Would you like to sell it?" I shook my head, but he continued. "I can give you a good price in rubles or dollars."

When I again said no, he then asked if I would like to exchange some of my money and offered me a price much higher than the official exchange rate. I asked him if he was at all concerned about being arrested, but he insisted that the authorities didn't bother him.

"But I thought this was illegal; isn't there a possibility of prison or fines?"

The man, who introduced himself as Serge, shook his head, and then continued the conversation, perhaps thinking the exchange might yet produce a customer for something he had. "Well, we are careful. If we carried around much more than forty dollars in cash or rubles there might be questions, and maybe a fine, but we don't. We approach only people who look like tourists; your camera gave you away. What Soviet would have something like that? Not many. So it's usually quite safe."

Serge further explained that they would often just trade, no money passing hands at all. He opened his satchel and showed me a few tins of caviar and some black lacquer boxes. "We might trade this for something you have; or if you wanted, you could buy it with dollars."

"How much?"

"Oh, perhaps five dollars for the caviar; fifty dollars for the box, much less than you would pay in the stores."

I did some quick calculating and figured that it was perhaps one-half or one-third less. Also, he was prepared to offer me twice as much in rubles for my dollars as I could get on the official exchange. If I both exchanged money and bought from him, I could end up increasing my purchasing power by four times. It was easy to see how tourists might be tempted to trade in the black market. But how, given those figures, could he and his friends make a profit?

"There's nothing much to buy in the Soviet shops, and what is there is very expensive," Serge said. "So people are eager to purchase from the foreign currency shops, and if I can get dollars, then I can ask foreign friends to go in and buy what I want. Or if I can obtain things that people want and are hard to get through normal channels, such as your camera, they will pay me extra. I can offer you a good price because I know they will pay me even more."

Serge was speaking so freely; wasn't he concerned about the possible dangers of being overheard? I know I would have been were I in his position. But as I glanced around, no one appeared to be paying any attention to us.

"What kinds of things do you usually get for people?" I wondered.

Serge went on. "Stereos, cameras, VCRs, appliances, that sort of thing. Foreign goods are so much better, and I find the tourists very receptive."

Then Serge asked to look at my camera. For a moment I hesitated, thinking I might soon be parted from it. However, deciding to take the risk, I tentatively held it out to him, the strap still around my neck, and as he turned it in his hands I thought ironically of how I would never chance such an inspection in the middle of a U.S. city. We had been assured there was very little crime and that we needn't be concerned about robberies and muggings, but I was secretly relieved when he handed the camera back.

Serge seemed to sense my thoughts and reassured me.

"You don't have to worry. Too bad you don't want to sell."

He took the cans of caviar and the lacquer boxes that his friends were holding and put them back in his satchel.

"How much do you usually make doing this?" I asked him.

"I can turn a profit of about 150 rubles a day. I make about 2,000 rubles a month."

It was considerably more than the ordinary worker made. Serge had become involved in the black market in his last year of public school through some older friends because it seemed like an easy way to make money.

"The penalties, if we're caught, are not very great," he continued. "I might be fined a few hundred rubles, which I can easily afford, so it makes good business sense, wouldn't you say? I live very well; I have a large apartment with a stereo, a color TV, and video equipment, and I can afford to travel whenever I want. Why shouldn't I do this? I consider this a good way to live, and I supply goods that people want."

From his point of view his argument made perfect sense. He was helping to provide goods in a system where there was an imbalance of supply and demand, and he could become rich, even a millionaire, by Soviet standards. However, many Soviets considered these people the dregs of society who mock or even endanger their socialist system by making so much money and doing so little work. So was what he was doing right or wrong? The question is still being debated, although gradually some forms of entrepreneurship and sales are being accepted. Unfortunately, I didn't have time to discuss this further with Serge because my group arrived. We said goodbye.

It was much quieter on the metro later at night. We decided to see a few more stations along the Ring Line and then had an easy, peaceful ride home.

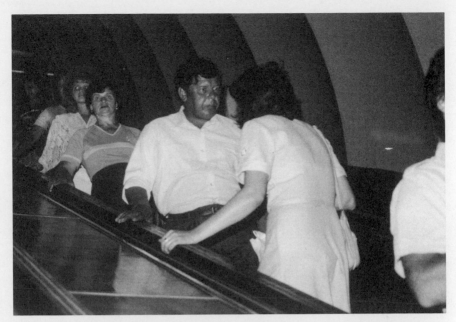

Metro — Leningrad

Playground — Leningrad

Market — Vilnius

Shop Window — Vilnius

Bridesmaid — Vilnius

Storefront — Minsk

Memorial — Khatyn

Concert — Gorky Park

Arbat Street — Moscow

Street Scene — Minsk

St. Basil's — Moscow

GUM Department Store — Moscow

Children's Peace Art

Young Pioneers — Moscow

Unloading Buses — Kiev

The beach at Kiev

CHAPTER 13

A Look at the New Society through the Eyes of Soviets

Our first day in Moscow was like a series of snapshots, each offering a glimpse of the many facets of this city.

Before breakfast, we visited a Russian Orthodox church near our hotel. To get there, we followed a narrow side street that turned into a dirt trail, and it felt like walking into an old Russian village with its small country church. Inside, amidst icons of holy family figures and saints, mostly older women were singing, kneeling, and lighting candles.

"They seem to have such a strong faith," Rowenna said as we walked outside. "It's as if they keep alive the traditions of Old Russia."

There was a kind of turning point going on in the role of the church in the U.S.S.R.—one more sign of the transformation taking place in Soviet society. Shortly before our arrival there had been a Millennium Celebration of one thousand years of Christianity in Russia, signaling to people that they could freely practice their religion as they wished. The Christian church occupies a central position in Russian history, having its initiation in the eleventh century when the Russians adopted the books, doctrine, music, paintings, monastic system, and even the architectural style that characterized the church in the West.

Contrary to the image many people have of the Soviet Union

135

as an irreligious, atheistic country, there are churches and temples representing many faiths, including Islam, Judaism, the many Christian religions with Catholicism dominating in Lithuania and the Ukraine, and millions of adherents to the Eastern or Russian Orthodox church. One highlight of our trip occurred in Leningrad when some of the churchgoers in our group met a woman who was part of an active religious community and whose small group had been given an 1870 chapel to fix up and use as a working church. The state was both recognizing them and preparing to donate money as well.

This was revolutionary, since the official Soviet position discouraged religious practice. Because many people still had reservations about letting others know they went to church, and open acknowledgment of it might still interfere with a successful career in the Party, we were warned against taking pictures in the churches we visited. "People consider this a private part of their lives. Just be sure to ask before taking photographs."

In the old cemetery next to the church, we found more reminders of the past. The cemetery was wild and overgrown, with small headstones peeping up out of the brambles. Colorful flowered wreaths were placed on some of the headstones, and on others there were pictures of gentle Russian faces.

There was a restful calm about the place, and for a few moments we felt stopped in time and space, oblivious to the busy world of Moscow all around us.

I had arranged to meet Yelena, who was also a writer, at Betty's suggestion. We set up the meeting for outside the hotel, and as our tour had run a little late, Jennifer and I now raced up the steps to look for her. We spotted her almost immediately, introduced ourselves, and led her into the hotel.

Yelena seemed very jumpy and unsure of her acceptance in this tourist setting, and as she told us her story over lunch, we soon understood why. At one time she had held a teaching position, but after a spat with her superiors she had lost her job and had spent the past fifteen years trying to get it restored to her. Not having a regular job made living within the bureaucracy much more difficult, such as getting permission for certain activities, including travel out of the country. As a result, she had experienced years of anger and frustration, all, according to Yelena, because she had upset someone in the bureaucracy.

"My problems started fifteen years ago when I gave a talk on one of my hobbies, art in the nineteenth century. I was invited to give a talk at a conference, but the authorities at my place of employment said I had no right to speak on this subject because I was a teacher of English and not an historian. I argued my position and they fired me.

"I contacted lawyers who said those who fired me were in the wrong because they violated our laws of work, which protects workers from being fired in one day; there are supposed to be hearings, meetings, a chance to talk and work things out. As if this weren't enough, they then lost some of my documents.

"I have complained. I have written to the Party, to attorneys, to trade unions, and to the government outlining my situation. But, generally, if you have a problem with an official organization, you can write anywhere you want and nothing will be resolved. They have the last word."

Yelena now made a living by giving private English lessons, doing occasional translations, and writing. She showed us a novel she had written about her family, which had just been translated into English.

She then spoke of her hopes for the future. "I look forward to change. At the Party Congress there was much discussion about recognizing the dignity of the individual; there seems to be more awareness about people's rights. This should help eradicate the kinds of problems I have been encountering; the Congress even acknowledged that people's complaints had not been acknowledged. As Gorbachev says, the rights people get are not a gift from the government, but the natural moral right of any person."

Yelena felt there would also be more respect for people's privacy. She welcomed the new openness and predicted positive change in a variety of areas. "It was decided at the Party Congress that there should be privacy for letters and telephone conversations, admitting that these were monitored. Perhaps money will now go toward more productive ventures.

"There will also be more freedom in art and literature. At one time the government considered these areas political and felt they had to exercise control. Now they are easing up, and we can talk more publicly about our ideas. The intellectuals think we can go forward now because our writers and poets are being returned to us, as is the truth about our past."

Understanding these truths helped clear the way for the future, Yelena thought. "It's like a cleansing. If we can speak of the darkness, the evil deeds committed, then perhaps they will not reoccur. We have been through seventy years of slavery since the Revolution; during those years, many talented and brave people perished, as in the purges of Stalin. But since now those horrors can be published, we can begin to breathe again. If Gorbachev did only this—gave us back our best writers and thinkers—and did nothing for the economy, I would be forever grateful."

Our thoughts turned to the economic changes in the wind, and we discussed some problems facing the Soviet consumer. "One of the first things that needs changing is the rude attitude of the shop girls," Yelena said. "They feel overly important because they get a salary whether they work or not, and they probably can't be fired. As a result they tend to be inconsiderate in dealing with customers. Gorbachev says education should change this. He feels people should be treated with courtesy and be able to make their purchases more quickly."

I agreed, describing my own experience in a *beryozka* shop where a dozen of us were in line and only one cash register was open. Meanwhile, several shop girls sat behind other cash registers casually talking. When I asked them to open up another line they just shook their heads, though when I announced that our bus was about to leave they ushered me to the head of the line.

"That's very typical," Yelena said.

Another problem in many Soviet stores, as Yelena complained, was the system of making purchases. First, you explained what you wanted to the clerk and she would put your item aside and give you a receipt. You then took the receipt to a cashier to pay and get it stamped, then returned to the original clerk to pick up your purchase. With this process ordinary shopping might easily take twenty minutes per item. Apparently Soviets put up with such inefficiency because it offered people work. I felt it pointed up the different priorities of our two countries; in the U.S. we would focus on making the system more efficient.

If the hoped-for new changes occurred, Yelena anticipated positive results for consumers and for the economy as a whole. For example, once there were no more market restrictions and people could get what they wanted at reasonable prices, that might be the end of the black market. The new cooperatives would play an important part in this economic transformation, too. In fact, already people welcomed the increasing variety of goods and services they offered, and Yelena was convinced this new spirit of entrepreneurship would grow, as it has.

"We all like the cooperatives because they will force prices down through competition, and also because family members and friends can work together as equal partners. It's not quite like capitalism since we can't hire outside workers, but it rouses the competitive spirit and encourages initiative and incentives such as higher quality and better service."

"It all sounds very exciting," Jennifer said. "You are all living through very historic times. What do you think the outcome will be?"

"There is resistance from those who don't want to work harder, from organizations that don't like the idea of lowering their prices, or officials afraid of losing their power. But there is pressure to move forward and to overcome the inertia that stands in the way of progress. The need for official organizations to be more responsive to change was also acknowledged at the Party Congress. I think that as people see the changes are good, even stimulating, they will be more and more receptive. Besides, this time there is no going back." At the time others might not have agreed with her certainty of the future, but her words proved to be prophetic.

We walked Yelena to the door and waved to her as she left the hotel. We wondered, with the new changes, would things change for Yelena, too?

The process of making a phone call in the Soviet Union is not always an easy task. I discovered this while attempting to set up some meetings for the following day. First of all, the system was frequently overloaded; then, the beeps and purrs on the line sounded so similar, it was hard to know if I was getting a ring, a busy signal, or still not getting through to an outgoing line. Once through, I often didn't get a response (message machines are rare) or ran into the language barrier. I also ended up with a lot of *nyet doma's*, meaning "not here" or "not at home."

After two hours, though, I managed to set up one meeting with the U.S.S.R.-U.S.A. Friendship Society, where fortunately most of the people in the office spoke English. I arranged an appointment to call someone the next day at the Soviet Peace Committee to schedule a meeting for our group, and left a message for someone about publishing my game, although I wasn't sure that it would ever reach him.

When I reported my frustrations to Betty at dinner, she laughed and said, "Welcome to the Moscow telephone system," then disclosed similar difficulties in setting up meetings for us. "It's just one of those things you get used to. You need persistence."

Betty had arranged for a party after dinner in her room, and like many Soviet parties it involved more serious discussion than is typical of American gatherings. Her friend Anton, a doctor from Leningrad, and his friend, Irina, had come to meet us and debate the changes taking place in the Soviet system. A year before, this discussion would have been unthinkable, but now they felt free to speak their minds.

Irina began the evening by telling us what she thought was one of the most positive changes—a blending of science, ecology, computers, work, family life, and entrepreneurship in a new organization.

"It's a group in Moscow which has big plans and blessings from the government, and they are involved in five different projects. Its purpose is to encourage an international exchange of ideas.

"First, they are creating a center for the gathering and dissemination of information of all kinds, particularly scientific, and all nations will be invited to participate. Our scientists are eager to share ideas with other scientists from all over the world. Secondly, an ecology park near Moscow will provide an in-depth education about the world's ecology and seek resolutions to current environmental problems. Additionally, there will be an international computer club, a complex devoted to living a healthy life in today's society, and scale models of cities designed to help children, and all of us, understand how cities work."

Irina named several organizations in the U.S. that were already behind the project, sounding like an excited marketing director. She had hopes of opening an office in Leningrad to support the projects. Soon, however, the conversation turned to power politics.

At this time, the distribution of power in the Soviet Union was divided between two key positions—the head of state, who was the chairman of the Presidium of the Supreme Soviet of the U.S.S.R., and the general secretary of the Communist Party Central Committee, who was the most powerful person in the

Soviet Union. When we were there, Gorbachev occupied the general secretary position, though subsequently his position became even stronger when he also took over as the chairman of the Presidium.

Gaining some background on these political roles before our trip helped us to understand the revolutionary change Gorbachev was about to propose: combining the heads of the government and of the party into one position, which made his role even stronger so that he could implement still further changes to transform the society over the years ahead.

We came to understand that although Gorbachev has certainly played a key role in guiding the Soviet Union into a process of transformation, he also has been responding to historical processes at work within the Soviet Union leading to a need to readjust the system. For example, we learned about the great economic difficulties the Soviet Union has been experiencing and its need to find ways to improve its economy, making it more productive and efficient by bringing in new technologies and management and marketing ideas developed outside the Soviet Union.

The historial background we assimilated also helped us to intelligently listen to the fascinating debates we heard about the changes the Soviet Union was just starting to experience. It quickly became apparent that there was no standard party line, no agreement on either side as to what was happening or what should happen. *Glasnost* led to a diversity of opinion—conservative as well as liberal. We experienced the excitement of many discussions about what could or should be and a sense of adventure that this change was happening right now. By thinking and speaking about it, the people were helping to shape that change.

Irina began talking about what she felt was wrong with the new reorganization program in the government.

"The whole idea behind the Party Congress and the Party's reorganization was to divide the power between the Soviet Councils, which run the local and national governments, and the Party. Yet now it seems the Party will participate even more in the government because the highest official at the local and national levels is now supposed to be a Party member. So it would seem that a non-Party member can't be at the top of the government anymore. And I don't think that's right, because Gorbachev talks about democratization—and in a real democracy, you can choose all of the highest officials in an election."

Anton, more of a conservative, disagreed.

"No, no. I think this change is a good thing, because it means the Party will now be held more responsible for its actions. I think this will occur, because the Party's power will now be officially acknowledged. And there is still an opportunity for democracy in that we will have a chance to oust people who aren't capable, through elections or impeachment. But at the same time, I think it is good that the Communist Party is finally gaining the full measure of power granted to it through our Constitution."

"Then we should change our Constitution now," Irina said, arguing in favor of future change. "I think we shouldn't just be limited to voting among members of the Communist Party for our top leadership. It's much fairer, I think, if we can choose anybody in the community."

Yet, Anton still argued staunchly for keeping the old ways, claiming that people didn't really want or need more democracy. He gave an example from the medical institute where he worked.

"Supposedly, we can elect whomever we want as the leader of our institute. But ninety-five percent of the people elect the same leader again and again, although no one likes him. Even though we can vote for a different candidate, no one thinks to do so, because we are used to voting for him. I do this myself. And at least he carries out his task. This shows that people think it's easier to continue with things as they are. It's just human nature to feel comfortable with keeping things the same way. You are seeking to change human nature. Maybe in some places like Lithuania, where there's a strong nationalist spirit, a real streak of independence, people have more of a vision for the future. But I think we have had a long tradition of accepting things as they are. I think most people don't really want to work hard for money, but would prefer to do less and get a smaller salary, because it's easier that way. They prefer stability, authority, and strong leadership to change."

"No, no, not anymore," Irina shot back. "I think you will see. Things are changing. People are beginning to stir. There's a new mood just emerging, and I think Gorbachev is nurturing that. People are starting to want a more democratic way of life, and I think it's time we educated people about the benefits of democracy. And I believe that's starting to occur. You'll see. You'll be left behind in the past. Even the conversation we're having now, a couple of years ago this couldn't occur. But now things are changing, and they will change even more. Just wait and see."

(Irina's words were certainly prophetic. As this book went to press in February, in one of the biggest political rallies since the Bolshevik Revolution, more than 100,000 people demonstrated outside the Kremlin walls on the eve of the meeting of the Central Committee, calling for an end to the Communist one-party monopoly. At Gorbachev's urging, Communist leaders voted to abolish one-party rule, allowing the Soviet Union freedom to have a multi-party system for the first time in over seventy years. And now still other changes are occurring, such as the passage of new laws to allow private property, set up free enterprise zones, and encourage Soviet and foreign joint ventures. Even McDonald's and Pizza Hut have come to the Soviet Union!)

And so the discussion went—Anton arguing for the strengthening of the Party he saw developing and the preservation of the old system, Irina for the strengthening of the new democracy she saw emerging, though she feared it might be trampled because it could be such a fragile thing, despite the new openness that now allowed her to argue for what she thought.

Though nothing was ultimately resolved, the discussion

itself reflected the new spirit of openness and democratization in the Soviet Union, and when it was over, despite their opposite interpretations and opinions, Anton and Irina were still the best of friends.

"We always argue like this," Irina said. "He thinks my position is a feminist one because I want to diffuse the power, and I tease him for being a traditional power-hungry male."

"To the new independence," toasted Betty.

In turn, we each held up our glasses to make a toast.

"To love and life."

"To peace and friendship."

"To an end to war and misunderstandings."

"To continued close ties between our groups."

"To future work together on creative projects."

"To the success of *glasnost* throughout the Soviet Union and the world."

CHAPTER 14

Visions of a World without War

The next morning began with another round of phone calls, some of them made en route to my meeting with the U.S.S.R.-U.S.A. Friendship Society. People on the street were generous when I tried to get change for the phone, which cost two kopeks (about three cents) a call. Each time I stood at the phone booth holding the large three-kopek piece which was too big, someone would quickly stop and give me a two-kopek piece, refusing to take my money. With their help and the persistence Betty had advised me to exercise, I was able to schedule the meetings I wanted for later in the day.

The U.S.S.R.-U.S.A. Friendship Society is housed in a massive yellow building behind a big iron gate. I traversed the courtyard and entered a spacious, though dark, lobby with a heavy stone spiral staircase off to one side. As I waited for the elderly receptionist to announce my arrival, a man in a dark suit appeared, pointed to a couch, and asked me to wait. "A few minutes," he said, tapping his watch.

After several minutes, Sergei Romanov, the secretary of the society, descended the spiral staircase, introduced himself, and asked me to follow him upstairs. He led me to a small conference room where we met his boss, Vadim Zhdanovich, the deputy executive secretary of the society.

We talked about their exchange programs with various U.S.

organizations. The programs had been in existence since 1985, growing along with the interest in democratization, and now, with *glasnost*, they hoped for opportunities to plan more exchanges.

"Our exchanges are between ordinary people and contribute to peace and the spread of ideas," Vadim said. "As more people participate, more stable bilateral relationships will build as a result of the trust and personal relationships that develop between hundreds of Soviets and Americans."

The exchanges had included a series of annual Soviet-American conferences in which well-known figures and government officials discussed areas of potential cooperation, such as cultural programs bringing together well-known performers.

"Our last conference was in Chautauqua, New York, and two hundred Soviets stayed in American homes. This year we'll have a conference in the Soviet Union, and Americans will be hosted by Soviet families. We try to involve a broad mix of people; we invite top officials in order to establish a sense of stability, people who have an interest in the U.S. or who are in scientific and economic research, and representatives of youth and educational institutions."

Vadim explained that the organization has chapters throughout the Soviet Union, including one at Moscow University. Groups involved in the exchanges, both in the U.S. and the Soviet Union, included the National Council for American-Soviet Friendship, a U.S. organization in existence since 1942; the Committee for Soviet Youth; the Soviet Women's Committee; the All-Union Council of Trade Unions and various other trade unions, and the American-Soviet Cinema Initiatives group. Additionally, there were exchanges among clergy of various denominations.

Vadim and Sergei were optimistic about the future and predicted that our two countries would come closer together. "We hope for further developments in cultural exchanges, including seeing more of each other's museums and theaters, and the elimination of stereotypes on both sides."

We shook hands, and Sergei gave me directions to my next

meeting. "It's just a stroll to the square, and then you can take the microbus."

—━━━━━━—

My "stroll" ended up being a mile and taking half an hour, since the Soviets are more used to walking than are Americans, who are apt to hop in the car even for short distances. But I found I enjoyed the experience—one more chance of doing it the way the Soviets do.

Soon I was on one of these Moscow microbuses which carry up to a dozen passengers to destinations not on the routes of regular buses. Several hundred of them supplement the city's bus and trolley lines. With over 600 routes on my map, I was amazed that people actually found their way around, and decided that asking—language barrier and all—would be more helpful than trying to puzzle through the map. "Does this bus to go Komsomolskaya Pravda?" I asked, repeating several times the name of the well-known Party newspaper for youth.

"Da," came the reply from several people, accompanied by rapid nods. One woman who spoke a little English indicated that I should follow her. At the end of the line she nudged me off and pointed to a low concrete building with the words Komsomolskaya Pravda over the doors.

The man I was meeting, Gennady Alferenko, had been involved in several Soviet-American joint ventures, including the marketing of Ben and Jerry's Ice Cream in the Soviet Union, and I thought he might help me find a Soviet producer for my game. He had asked me to meet him at the building's entrance promptly at 12:30 P.M. However, since I arrived a few minutes early, I decided to go in and find my way to his office. A bad idea. A police guard stopped me at the stairs.

I repeated Gennady's name several times, thinking that a receptionist could just let him know I was here or that someone would show me to his office. The officer looked at me blankly.

"Pass, pass," he kept saying, and when I managed to convey that I had no pass, his reply was a simple "Nyet." I went back outside to wait.

Precisely at 12:30 P.M. Gennady appeared, looking not at all like my image of a tough Soviet negotiator and deal maker. He looked more like someone I might expect to run into on a college campus, with his gentle hippie appearance and slightly long hair. He was younger than I expected, perhaps thirty, and was dressed casually in sports shirt, jeans, and denim jacket.

"Hello, have you been waiting long?" he asked, holding out his hand to greet me. "We'll have to get a pass for you." We went up to the same guard who had told me "Nyet," and in a matter of minutes we had my pass.

Gennady's office was near the end of a long hall of small offices, and filled with magazines, books, and newspapers. He introduced me to his three assistants, all of whom shared the office, then invited me to lunch in the newspaper's cafeteria.

He had previously worked in Siberia as a geophysicist and had moved here because he wanted a change. "I found a job on this newspaper, and I like it because there's practically no bureaucracy. I can write an article and it immediately reaches 18 million people."

Besides working on the paper, Gennady looked for ways to encourage individual creativity. "Our old-style organizations promote the group and are very entrenched in their ways. I feel there's a need to push individuals to find their own talents, and also to create joint ventures between American and Soviet companies. I've set up an enterprise in support of this—now possible with the new laws permitting new enterprises and cooperatives."

He described how he had made the connections for Ben and Jerry's and for another game about peace, and promised to speak to some of his associates about my game.

When I told him about some of my other projects, I was surprised by his level of interest. He said he might be interested in having my book, *Mind Power: Picture Your Way to Success in*

Business, translated into Russian. I hadn't imagined that the Soviets would be overly interested in creative visualization or in techniques for business success, but Gennady was enthusiastic, saying the Soviets were eager to learn whatever they could about new business methods and entrepreneurship.

He also showed interest in my book on shamanism, saying there was a revival of interest throughout the Soviet Union in exploring traditional roots. He told me to contact his friend, a doctor who had set up the Center for Shamanic Studies. "He is using shamanism for healing purposes and will be interested in your book."

My next meeting was with the Soviet Peace Committee, and Gennady offered to have his driver take me there. We said our goodbyes, and his assistant escorted me to a big black four-door sedan where the half-dozing driver quickly snapped to attention. I slid into the back seat and we roared off.

I felt like a celebrity as we raced along—there was something special about being in a private car with my own driver, especially in a place where there were very few cars at all. For those brief minutes, after days of walking and taking buses and metros, I luxuriated in this feeling, imagining the lives of Party officials with their special perks.

My reverie was abruptly interrupted by a police siren behind us. My driver pulled over and the officer motioned for him to come back to the police car. I wasn't sure if he was getting a ticket, and I couldn't ask because he didn't speak English, but I guessed this was what was happening as he pulled out his ID and afterwards drove at a much slower pace. Apparently, it seemed, even the more privileged have to follow the rules.

The Soviet Peace Committee was located appropriately on the Prospect Mira. Because the director was on vacation, I was greeted by her assistant, Natalya. We joined the others in my group; then Natalya escorted us to a conference room to meet Tanya, head of a group called the Center for Creative Initiatives and a member of the board of directors of the Peace Committee, and four girls of fourteen or fifteen who worked with her on her various projects. They were seated on one side of a huge octagon-shaped conference table.

Tanya was a teacher of economics at Moscow State University, and she related her activities with the Peace Committee, which primarily involved children's projects. The first was a program called Peace Child, where groups of American and Soviet children stage a free-form drama all over the world about peace. The project was started when a group of American children came to the U.S.S.R. and performed a play by an American playwright who received his inspiration from an ancient tradition in which tribes at war exchanged children to guarantee the peace. An ex-NATO general in the U.S. heard about the play and suggested to his son-in-law, also a playwright, that he use his talent to promote peace. The result was Peace Child.

"It's a story of American kids who come to the Soviet Union," Tanya said. "Both sides have grown accustomed to hostile images of each other. Then circumstances cause one of the American kids to mingle with Soviet kids, and they become friends. Also, an American girl and a Russian boy fall in love in the story, finding it hard to part. Later we see them grown up, and both are committed to peace. There are different versions based on this main theme because we encourage the children to be creative with it. They often make these performances into musicals."

Tanya explained that the Peace Child program had been taken under the umbrella of the Soviet Peace Committee by the Center for Creative Initiatives, and that it had the support of the U.N. and other official groups. American children could come to the Soviet Union and join the play, along with Soviet children. The Americans pay for their transportation, but live in a camp paid for by the center. Their families could come as

well, again paying only for transportation; contributors from
both countries paid for their stay. Funds were tight, but it was
hoped enough money could be raised to keep the project going.

Tanya then described plans for a U.S./Soviet venture in
opening peace parks called Peaceland. One was scheduled for
Nashville, and another for Moscow. An organization in Nashville called Planet Earth was involved in finding land, and millions of dollars had been raised through the participation of
some big corporations such as Sony U.S.A.

"Architects from both our countries are designing the project together. There will be a hotel, complexes for meetings, and
a cinema and theater, because some projects will center around
making films and staging plays. We expect several thousand
people to be in the park at any one time. Although it is primarily
designed for children and their parents, anyone can come.

"We even have plans to make a film about the program. A
team of cameramen from the U.S. is planning to shoot a docu-
mentary, and some very talented and famous people are involved, all on a volunteer basis."

Tanya hoped to see these projects expand to include Third
World countries. She felt that a united U.S.-U.S.S.R. could
help to develop the Third World so that it would stop being an
arena for conflict.

Once again it was time to play my game, with Gert acting
as translator. The girls took it very seriously. They were well
informed about world events and eager to discuss Soviet-
American issues. Afterward I donated the game to the center,
and Tanya said they would play it at their next Peace Camp.

On the way home, we discussed what might happen if our
children were stimulated to think about peace earlier. The toy
manufacturers made all these games and toys to make war seem
like so much fun—couldn't they do the same for peace?

CHAPTER 15

The Many Faces of Moscow

At dinner, Betty recounted a somewhat Kafka-esque tale about our tickets to Kiev. There had been obstacles from the beginning arising from the fact that Nalya, her friend in Kiev, and not Intourist, was making the arrangements.

"The officials just aren't used to people within the U.S.S.R. setting up independent travel, so Nalya had trouble getting train tickets, hotel reservations, and a bus for a city tour. Finally she succeeded, only to find that our train tickets had been reversed: Instead of being written from Moscow to Kiev and back, they were written from Kiev to Moscow. Apparently, the ticket office clerk thought there must be a mistake, since Nalya was in Kiev."

Naturally, we all thought the tickets could just be changed, but Betty explained the difficulty in changing anything once it was done. Since there was no computer system for ticketing, a clerk couldn't make the change in a few minutes as we are used to, but had to locate the original order in the files and then find someone authorized to make the change. It usually takes about one week to issue tickets, and we had only twenty-four hours. At this late date there no longer might have been space left on the train.

So Nalya traveled to the central ticket office in Moscow to see if anything could be done. When she, Betty, and Kurt arrived there shortly after noon, there were perhaps fifty people in front of the door.

"It took hours," Betty said. "We were in line for an hour and it didn't even move. We knew we had to get in by five or it would be too late."

Kurt continued the story. "At four there were still twenty people in front of us. It seemed as if the door was locked, and no one knew what was happening. Had they closed the office? Was there any use in waiting? But everyone else stayed put, so we did too.

"Finally, at quarter to five the door opened and we were invited to come in. There was an explosion of people as everyone pushed up to the door, and even inside we were asked to wait in another line.

"When we finally reached the clerk, she said she couldn't change the tickets in such a short time. Perhaps that would have been the end of it, but Nalya was insistent. 'I must speak to someone else,' she said. 'You must let me speak to your supervisor.' Just when it looked like there would be a yelling incident, the clerk backed down.

"When the next person also said it was impossible, Nalya insisted on seeing someone else until we finally spoke to someone with enough power to change the ticket. Only because Nalya persisted did we succeed; it took a lot of courage."

"We have the tickets *to* Kiev for tomorrow night," Betty continued, "but we still don't know about coming back; it depends on getting space on the trains. We won't know until we are in Kiev, so we'll just have to flow with what happens in the meantime."

We left dinner wondering what it would be like to deal with the intricate workings of the Soviet bureaucracy on a day-to-day basis. "It's a little like trying to get a license at the DMV," Kurt said wryly, "or going to court and protesting a ticket. Dealing with any bureaucracy takes a long time; maybe the Soviets have a few more bureaucrats, but otherwise it's one more thing our two countries have in common."

After dinner, a few people in our group went off to the

Moscow circus, a gala extravaganza of bright lights, acrobats, clowns, lions, tigers, aerialists, and dancing bears. I joined Jennifer, Gert, and Sarah for a trip to the Arbat, a Soviet version of Greenwich Village. We had heard about it from the popular book, *Children of the Arbat*, by Anatoli Rybakof.

We arrived via metro at 8:00 P.M. to a street thronged with people. Artists had set up stands along the boulevard, closed to traffic for about a mile, and here and there tourists posed for portraits as people gathered to watch. Other artists stood beside paintings which leaned against or hung on sides of buildings, and folk singers plunked away on guitars and balalaikas. Lines of people snaked out of a few cafes selling soda and ice cream, while others window-shopped at stores selling books, clothing, paintings, and assorted souvenirs.

On a small wooden stage to one side, a group of younger teenagers dressed in denim jackets, T-shirts, and jeans were playing a tape of rock music. At intervals, one or two of the boys would start jerking, dancing, or spinning around on the floor, break-dance style.

Further along, a folk group had assembled and was starting to play. Within moments, loud Russian music blasted from an overhead window, drowning them out. The folk musicians soon gave up and moved on, and the Russian music quickly stopped. "That's nicer than shouting out of the windows to get them to stop," Jennifer mused.

I noticed that people here seemed to be more stylishly dressed. The women were wearing either jeans or fashionable blouses, sweaters, and skirts, and there was a trendiness in the men's fitted slacks, jeans, jackets, and T-shirts. Also, the atmosphere was loose—people lounged in doorways and squatted on steps, not permissable in most other areas.

"It's like another world," Jennifer said, "a place where people can come and be or do whatever they want. I wouldn't mind living here myself."

I thought about the contrasts of the day: the official diplomacy of the Friendship Society and the Peace Committee; the complications over the tickets; Gennady's entrepreneurial zest; the spontaneous, magnetic Arbat—like a scene from the American sixties alive in the Soviet Union today. It was a painting of many colors, crafted in many styles, creating a fascinating tapestry in its variety.

Our last day in Moscow went by quickly. At our morning meeting Betty described our options: a boat ride on the Moscow River; an art museum with modern Russian works; a pet market on the outskirts of town.

A few people went off to the pet market and later described it as an open-air market where people brought dogs, cats, parakeets, rabbits, and small hamsters, displaying them on leashes or in cages. I spent a few hours at a traveling exhibit of modern Russian art, highlighted by the long-unappreciated work of the Russian Impressionists. Then I went to Gorky Park.

Because of the movie *Gorky Park*, I imagined this would be a deeply mysterious place with an aura of the secret rendezvous about it, but it was nothing of the sort. Instead, it was a cheerful, festive place—a little like a spring day in Central Park with a carnival. In front of the entrance, a big marble gate flanked by tall marble columns, people were having their pictures taken in a small yellow-and-blue car with bright red trimming or beside a colorful centipede-like figure with three clown heads. Inside, pitchmen sold ice cream and creamy white candy cones or offered rides on donkeys and bicycles. There was a large ferris wheel and rides for kids in miniature airplanes and cars. Meanwhile, at bandstands scattered here and there, orchestras or singers performed in celebration of classical music day at the park. Elsewhere, there were areas for boating, sylvan groves with benches, and artists and folk singers much like the Arbat. Perhaps most impressive was the troupe of actors dressed like lords and ladies from the Middle Ages who rode through the park on horseback, like a caravan of pilgrims out of Chaucer, announcing their performance later that night.

Suddenly my attention was drawn to a tall building on a hill where a crowd gathered expectantly. The man at the entrance was yelling and gesturing like a circus barker. It looked like something amazing was about to begin, so I went in and took a seat. Below the audience was a large circular pit that looked like the inside of a wooden beer vat. A spotlight flashed on to illuminate the bottom of the pit, and after a few minutes a master of ceremonies walked out in a glittering white jacket and pants to announce that we were about to see two motorcyclists defy gravity. In a a burst of fanfare, the motorcyclists flew in as if they had been shot out of a cannon. They wore sparkly white jackets and red helmets, and began circling the pit, revving their motors to build up the tension in the crowd.

Finally, they began to climb the walls. One at a time they whirled around the bottom picking up speed, then suddenly climbed on an angle rising higher and higher until they were riding perpendicular to the floor. The crowd watched breathlessly. Then they shot down again to the ground. After performing their stunt several times, the crowd clapped in wild appreciation.

I walked out of the park thinking of that whirling image and of the Soviet people we had met. Initially, the task looked impossible, but the motorcyclists did it anyway, taking the risk of failing. They broke through difficult barriers and soared free, flying like sleek birds, showing what the human will can do. "Last year most of this trip would have been impossible," I remembered Betty saying. "We never could have met people in the way we are doing or talked so freely with them."

Like the cyclists, and the Soviets, we, too, were breaking through barriers with our citizen diplomacy, and like the circling image, we were all connected.

We had a special ceremony before we left Moscow—an appreciation party for Lena, whom we would be seeing for the last time. Lena had been much more than a guide—she had become our friend. From the beginning Lena had been always there for us, flexible and spontaneous, as when she took us on the metro tour during rush hour the day we arrived.

We gathered in Betty's room an hour before we had to leave for the train station, packing in closely on beds and chairs, while Lena sat in one corner looking angelic—her face framed by her long dark hair and white, high-collared blouse.

"We want to show our appreciation for all you have done for us," Betty said, handing her our group gift of a gold heart-shaped locket on a chain. Others handed her individual gifts of children's books, tapes, pictures, photos, peace posters, and various pins and *glasnost* buttons.

Looking a little overwhelmed by all these presents, she slowly put the locket around her neck. "This is all so unexpected," she said with tears in her eyes. Then she stood up and gave a little speech. "I am really touched. You have all been so generous, so kind. From the beginning I felt that this group was different: more curious, more out-reaching, more eager to understand, more interested in us. I had a group in the seventies like this; they came in a spirit of detente. But not since then have I seen anything like this, and when I try to tell people at work, they don't believe me. 'You make up stories,' they say. But I know, and I will always remember you."

It was a tearful moment as she led us to our Intourist bus— several of our new Soviet friends were waiting to pile on board with us, as they wanted to see us off at the train. Lena announced that another Intourist guide, Yuri, would meet us at the station.

"I would so like to be with you, but I must return to Leningrad tonight. Yuri will take care of you and make sure you get on the right train. The station is so busy; it can be quite confusing, as you will see."

The station was in fact a booming, buzzing center of activity. A huge, gothic-looking structure with a tall tower, it reminded me of the Empire State Building with two long concrete arms. Outside was the constant hustle of buses and taxis as people streamed in and out of the terminal like ants. Tired-looking families waited by piles of luggage. A family of Gypsies wearing bandannas camped in one doorway, and further down a soldier waited with his wife and daughter, who looked like a little angel in her white dress, knee socks, and long pigtail with a bright red bow.

Inside, the huge crowd resembled rush hour on the metros, but the station was much larger—more like a downtown street with shops. Along one side were small stalls with vendors; one woman even offered haircuts. There was also a good-sized games arcade filled mostly with young boys shooting intently at various targets.

As I walked through the arcade a boy of twelve or thirteen with a bag slung over his shoulder came over and asked if I would like to buy some caviar: "A good price, very nice." When I said no, he quickly disappeared into the crowd.

On a far side of the station was a kind of map room with several rows of glass cases, similar to those in museums. By pressing a button, Rolodex-like cards inside the cases could be maneuvered to show train and bus routes. I walked around for a few more minutes savoring the station's energy. It felt exhilarating, like being in the center of a pumping heart, the people like the blood circulating from chamber to chamber.

Finally it was time to rejoin the group. Yuri had arrived and safely conducted our luggage to the main train platform where five trains were lined up in a row like horses waiting at a gate, their dark blue coats gleaming. We formed a fire-fighter-type line to distribute the luggage to our compartments, and just as we were about to take off, Nalya hopped on.

"So now you are all set," said Yuri, obviously relieved that our Kiev connection had actually shown up. "I leave you in good hands. When you return, Intourist will arrange for someone to meet your train."

As the train pulled out, we crowded around the doors and waved to our friends. It reminded me of going off to camp when I was seven; the Soviets blowing kisses much like my parents had done so many years ago. Our sleeping compartments also invoked camp memories. We were traveling second class, which meant four to a compartment, two on the top and two on the lower berths.

Stowing our luggage was a bit like putting together a jigsaw puzzle—we had crawl spaces between the beds, around the top of the compartment, and under the lower bunks. There were also hanging net baskets next to each bed for small items. In first and third class the space allotment was the same, but in first class there were only two to a compartment, and in third class there were no doors. Since there were eighteen of us, Betty and Kurt shared their compartment with two Soviet factory workers on holiday. "Well, this is another good way to meet Soviets," Betty said.

Once settled, we bounded up and down the aisles like little kids, peering in compartments, taking pictures, looking out of windows at the countryside rolling by. Miles of apartment buildings, factories, trams, shops, and cluttered backyards gradually gave way to long stretches of open fields, stands of birches, and dense forests.

Meanwhile, we discovered the traditional Soviet custom of serving tea on trains. Every car had a big white boiler, or samovar, and the conductor brought us steaming tea with a large lump of sugar for just twenty kopeks (thirty-five cents) a glass.

The train ride provided many opportunities for citizen diplomacy. Carolyn went up and down the aisles with her Polaroid; Angela remembered the melody of a song she thought was Russian and asked the Soviet Armenians in an adjacent compartment if they knew it. They did, and she ended up leading a group of us in song. Jennifer, Gert, and I visited with a family from Moscow on their way to a month-long vacation with relatives in Kiev. Both husband and wife were teachers; he had just returned from teaching chemistry in Damascus. Their fourteen-year-old daughter hoped to be a teacher, and their son, sixteen, wanted to study engineering. Jennifer showed pictures of her own family and soon we were deep in conversation.

They could have been a typical suburban American family as they shared concerns about jobs, income, family, taxes, and their children's success. The man spoke proudly of their progress in school and how they already had plans for the future. He had recently moved his family from Kiev to Moscow because of more opportunities. We showed them our Kiev guidebook and they recommended several points of interest.

As we prepared to leave, the man pulled out three crisp new rubles. "I want you to have these," he said, giving one to each of us. "They are new rubles, mementoes of our conversation."

"Thank you so much," I said, putting it into my book. "I will mount it and put it on my wall at home," and as I said this I realized that's exactly what I would do.

After another hour we pulled in at a country station with a simple wooden station house in the distance. The path was lined with colorful flowers, and we poured out of the train eager to breathe the fresh air and supplement the food we had brought with the locally grown fruits and vegetables. However, as it turned out, we had only a five-minute stop and were just starting to make our purchases when the whistle blew. Charity, Helga, and Kurt were still standing next to the train as it started to roll. Startled, they turned and began to jog beside it as the train gathered speed. Kurt threw himself on, and Bill managed to grab onto Charity and pull her in, but Helga found herself stranded on the platform as our car hurtled past. When another car went by with the door open, she managed to leap on. Groaning and panting, she walked through car after car until she reached us.

"It was like going into another world," she told us, throwing herself onto her lower bunk. "The other cars don't have doors: I passed people having picnics, and groups of men without shirts passing around drinks and singing. It looked like a beach party."

We rumbled on, and as it grew dark, we were lulled to sleep by the clacking of wheels on the tracks.

PART VI

KIEV
Off the Beaten Track

CHAPTER 16

An Evening with a Student Youth Group

At six in the morning a knock on our compartment door announced we were nearing Kiev. We hurriedly stumbled around getting dressed and finishing the last of our food. A few minutes before seven, we pulled into the station.

Nalya's friend Aleksei, also a member of the local student U.S.S.R.-U.S.A. friendship group, was there to meet us. Although she had no connection to Intourist, Nalya had arranged for an Intourist bus, and we were soon on our way to the Hotel Tourista on the left bank of the Dnieper River, just across from the main part of town. It was similar to an Intourist hotel in size and accommodations, but this time we had to drag our own luggage upstairs.

After a quick lunch we were off for our city tour, which turned out to be considerably more informal than the Intourist tours we were used to. Our guide Marina led these only occasionally because she had a full-time job, and she spoke only Russian.

"But I'll be translating for her," Nalya said cheerfully.

Marina presented her city with a kind of down-home folksiness that combined fascinating folk tales about the founding and history of Kiev with a touch of irreverence. For example, when showing us a particular monument, she would recite the details and then might add something like, "But the local peo-

ple don't like this. They don't feel it represents the spirit or
style of Kiev."

Best of all were Marina's stories.

"Kiev was founded over fifteen centuries ago by three
brothers traveling downriver on a boat. When they saw our
beautiful hills, they decided to found a city, naming it Kiev
(which means "belonging to Kie") after the elder brother, whose
name was Kie. They named the two surrounding hills after the
other brothers, and gave their sister's name to the small river,
calling it the Luba. Now it is a city of over 2 million and the
third largest city in the Soviet Union after Leningrad and
Moscow."

As we crossed the bridge into the main section of Kiev,
Marina told us how Kiev changed from a pagan into a Christian
state.

"It happened one thousand years ago in the year 988. The
ruler in those days, Prince Vladimir, decided to introduce
Christianity, and he ordered the people to throw all their religious objects and pagan gods into the Dnieper. Then he had
them go into the water to be baptized on that very spot." She
pointed to a small white monastery with a green dome standing
on a small rise across the river. "He built the Vydubichi Monastery to show where the Christians obtained power over the
pagan god."

Marina had a habit of chiding whoever happened to be in
power at the time. As we passed an eleventh-century cathedral,
built in an ornate Byzantine style shortly after the Christian
conversion, she explained how the Christians procured money
to finance the expansion of their religion. "Because it was
customary to bury nobles and others in the monasteries, monks
would sell the cemetery ground to raise money. The closer the
grave was to the monastery, the more the person would have to
pay."

Later we passed a massive stone column projecting into the
sky, which Marina said was supposed to be a monument to the
motherland. "But everyone from Kiev hates this monument,"

she stated quite firmly. However, this dislike wasn't political. Rather, it was for artistic reasons. As Marina explained: "A monument to the motherland should express the feelings of a mother. It should be soft, gentle. But this huge thing going into the sky—does that suggest a mother to you?"

When we passed a monument dedicated to the reunion of Russia and the Ukraine featuring a large rainbow-shaped marble arch over two massive sculptures, Marina continued with her usual arch commentary. "It's a symbol of the Ukraine becoming a part of Russia in 1654, after the Russians helped liberate the Ukraine from the Lithuanians and the Poles. The rainbow bridge symbolizes joy, since rainbows appear just before the sun comes out. But many Kievians don't like this monument either because it's so big; it doesn't seem to capture the human feeling."

She also criticized the town's architecture. "It represents Stalin's time. Buildings were constructed on a grandiose scale to glorify the power of the state. People here feel these buildings don't represent their real spirit, for Ukrainians like a more ornate or a free-form look. The buildings represent the struggles the people went through—they had little equipment, worked very hard, and many died."

As we drove along, Jennifer commented, "I don't think this is the tour we would have had with Intourist."

Some of the places Marina took us had an off-the-beaten-track feel. We saw the parks and appreciated the lush greenery of Kiev as did most tourists, but we also visited a small chapel with a strikingly nontraditional feature. The chapel was once part of a functioning monastery, but as Marina explained, "In the 1940s during the war, many Catholic churches were destroyed, as was most of this area. This one has now been restored as an exhibition hall for ceramics." Then she took us around front to see its unusual cross: the image of an ordinary jacket with its arms outstretched. "This cross is very significant. Until a few years ago, no one could make or exhibit something as modern as this. It was all right to show traditional crosses—that was part of history. This one suggests the people's current faith."

The unique flavor of this tour was a fitting introduction to our independent journey to Kiev, where everything seemed unscheduled and more relaxed. Before, we had found ways to leave the tour in order to meet the people; now, the people we would normally have left the tour to meet were leading it!

That evening we went to a meeting of a student youth group called the Soviet-American Citizen Diplomacy Club. The members of this group would be our Kiev hosts, along with Nalya, and had worked out the arrangements for our tour; they would be joining us on most of our activities, giving us a very personal, inside look at Kiev.

Nalya picked us up at 8:00 P.M. After a short metro ride, we walked several blocks to a wooded park in the center of the city, then along a series of paths that wound through the park to the clubhouse. Two dozen people were waiting to greet us, most of them students in their twenties. They were dressed for a party and had festively decorated the main room with balloons and pictures of children's art about peace. A large table was set with cakes, cookies, and tea.

The students invited us to sit down, and a man named Boris read a brief opening speech:

> Dear Friends. We, the members of the Soviet-American Citizen Diplomacy Club, are happy to meet you here at our premises. Today we have an excellent opportunity to understand each other and ourselves. We are all of the human family, and our Earth is our common home. So we hope that this meeting will turn out to be one of great sharing, new experiences, and mutual love.

We want you to feel at home, be relaxed and comfortable. Let this table be the table of friendship and understanding. You are welcome to tea and communications.

Pointing to the table, he added, "Help yourself."

At once, we all began moving around and mixing. Jennifer talked with a woman who worked as a typist for a minister of economics. Gert found some common interests with a man wearing an I Love New York T-shirt. They talked about his hopes to visit the U.S., especially New York and California. Betty found some students involved in repairing and preventing damage to computers and steered them over to Charles.

Meanwhile, I showed my *Glasnost* game to a few people. Alyosha, who was studying to be a teacher, was especially interested in one of the questions on education: "In the Soviet Union, higher education is free, and the students have to pass tough exams to qualify. What do you think of this idea?" After his friend Misha translated the question for Alyosha's wife Anya, who knew very little English, Alyosha replied. "I like it that school is free, but I don't think the exams are always fair, because a person might know more than he can present on the exam. Yet, he is judged solely on this."

Anya cut in, speaking to Misha in Russian. "She wants to say," Misha translated, "that though there is much stress associated with these exams and people may not like them, she feels the use of exams is fine for determining someone's achievement. She also says that most people in the Soviet Union feel this way."

Alyosha disagreed. "I don't like the way the exam separates people into two tiers—those who can go on and those who cannot. And it's all based on one exam. Suppose I can't show all I know when the time comes? I may not be able to go on, though I have the ability, and that isn't right."

"When you pass, you will feel differently," Anya through Misha said.

Then Boris stopped by, glanced at a few game questions, and answered one about the pros and cons of our two systems by giving a little speech.

"You see," he began, "I am just an ordinary person, and I speak only from my own feelings. But when the bureaucrats speak, they give only their organization's position, and they and their groups can be quite resistant to change. Our system doesn't reward risk-taking. In the Soviet Union we try to organize all things according to an overall ideology, but that can make the system quite rigid and keep it from responding to the day-to-day problems which arise. Thus, these problems continue, and the results, as you have seen, are a lack of consumer goods, long lines, shortages, and high prices.

"We envy you some of your advantages because your system is more flexible, more responsive to change and progress. You are more open to taking risks. Yet, we are also aware of your problems such as the homeless and the poor, the people who do not make it in your system, as opposed to here, where the state takes care of everyone's basic needs. We may lack many of the material advances and complain about too much bureaucracy, but in some ways we feel more secure."

Boris spoke of the value Soviets place on friendship. "The word of a friend is usually taken very seriously. We may not be sure about what the officials are saying, or about what the newspapers are saying, but our friends are like anchors when so much else is uncertain. But then, we are brought up to be part of a team."

"We value friendship too," Susan said, "but in the U.S. friends are often quite casual with each other. When they say something, it's not always clear that they will follow through."

Just then, we heard people in the next room singing folk songs. Petr, the man in the I Love New York T-shirt, was playing his guitar and Nalya was sitting beside him, singing. She sang some American folk songs—"We Shall Overcome," "You are My Sunshine," "The Man From Galilee"—and then sang traditional songs from the Ukraine. One told the story of a man who wanted to ride off to marry his prospective wife, but he had constant delays and his bride angrily demanded an explanation. First he told her his mother told him not to go, "but I didn't worry about that." Then his father told him not to go, "but I didn't worry about that either." Then his sister took his saddle so he couldn't ride his horse. Finally, his other sister found it, so "Here I am at last. Please, I ask you, be my bride!" And she said yes.

Another was a plaintive tale of a girl who wanted to go with a man to another country to be his wife, but he said, "No, I already have a wife." She said, "Then I'll come and be your sister," but he said, "No, I already have a sister." So she said, "Well then, I'll be a friend," but he said no. Finally she said, "I'll be a stranger," and he said, "No, I don't want you for a stranger." So what was she to be? The upshot, as I gathered from Nalya later, was that the relationship was sadly doomed from the start.

After perhaps another hour of talking, singing, taking photos, and exchanging names and addresses, it was time to go. Several group members—Petr, Nalya, Boris, Alyosha, and Anya among them—walked us to the metro. As we strolled about a mile along dark, tree-lined streets, we divided into small clusters, two or three of us around each Soviet.

Boris, who was a painter, described his life as an artist in Kiev, and spoke about work, housing, and travel. Like the other people we met, he played down his special skills and abilities, as if to stress humility and the ultimate importance of the group and his being a part of it. I asked him if he ever considered going to Moscow to paint, since I understood it was the center for the arts.

"It is true Moscow is the center, and any very talented artist will most likely be invited to go there. However, I feel it is better to stay where you are and establish a reputation first."

"Do new trends and discoveries ever start in another city and then spread to Moscow?" I asked, explaining that many U.S. trends originate in California.

"We do have a surgeon from Kiev who is known all over the country. But, generally, if a person desires nationwide recognition it is best to go to Moscow."

Due to housing shortages in the Soviet Union, Boris had experienced some difficulties getting a place to live in Kiev after graduating in art. According to the law, as a young specialist he was supposed to be able to obtain a place from the state within three years in the city where he obtained work. Apparently the system operated on the assumption that people would have somewhere to stay in the meantime, and in fact many young people lived at home after finishing school until their names came up on the waiting list for state flats.

This could take a long time, depending on availability and the number of people who received priority treatment. Veterans of foreign wars were supposed to have priority, but those sufficiently talented or possessing needed skills would often have the way eased for them. According to Boris, the normal waiting time was usually one or two years, but some people ended up waiting many years longer, generally making their own ad hoc arrangements, such as trading apartments in different cities or doubling up with a friend or relative.

Although it was possible to engage in an exchange with someone who had a flat in another city by consulting publications that listed flats, people more often dealt with the problem as Boris himself had—they paid someone a lot of money for a flat. As Boris described it, there was a flourishing unofficial market in flats helping the flow of state-owned housing. Though it was illegal and the state had recently cracked down on landlords renting their apartments this way, even bringing some cases to court, they soon stopped their campaign because they realized it could contribute to people being homeless. So there was little risk now of legal penalties.

"On the unofficial market a flat can cost seventy to one hundred rubles," Boris observed. "It is high, and I end up paying about half my salary, but I am content because I have a home. And my landlord is content to be rid of a place he no longer needs and is perhaps paying a high rent to someone else."

In many cases people needed to leave their homes only temporarily; they might take an interim job in another city, or a man being called for military service might send his young family to stay with his parents for a while. Renting their flat on the unofficial market meant both extra income and not having to face another long wait for housing upon their return.

However, anyone renting illegally would have an unregistered passport, which could create difficulties in gaining access to state services—the same problem Olga in Leningrad faced until she found her job. Because Boris had a job and could obtain a certificate for services from his employer, he was covered. But a person still looking for work would not be.

I was curious about this internal passport system that registered people for overall social control, and asked Boris if people needed to carry passports when traveling within the Soviet Union.

"In most traveling, no. We need our passports only when flying from one city to another. On trains, the authorities never check; however, I usually carry my passport with me in case I decide to go by plane en route."

We arrived at the metro and discussed our plans for the following day before parting. Alyosha and Anya wanted to invite us for tea and cakes; Boris suggested a visit to the museum of Ukrainian art; Petr offered to take a group of us to the beach; Nalya proposed a walk through downtown.

We hugged good night, then rode home thinking of the possibilities. There were so many choices, and it was delightful to have the students as our personal guides—through the city and into their way of life.

CHAPTER 17

A Day at the Beach and Exploring Kiev

The next day was one of the high points of the trip for me. While most of the group went shopping in downtown Kiev, Betty, Rowenna and her two children, Belinda and Darla, and I went with four of the students—Ilya, Petr, Gleb, and Fyodor—to the beach. It was a chance to relax and to experience the beach, Soviet-style.

Wearing bathing suits under our clothes and toting thermoses, bottles of Coke, notebooks, and other items for a day at the beach, we took the metro to the left bank of the Dnieper River, then walked across a bridge to a small island. As we gazed in either direction, we saw lines and lines of bodies and beach chairs under a warm sun, and several partitioned changing rooms. A few people, mostly children and teenagers, splashed in the water. A few colorful umbrellas poked up here and there.

The students knew of a more private beach, so we followed them onto a high path that led through a wooded area. Down in a ravine two older women in housedresses appeared to be tidying up the area with whisk brooms. After hiking about a half mile, we arrived at a cozy, isolated beach shaded by the surrounding woods. A scattering of people napped on blankets or read, basking in the sun and the gentle cool breeze.

Ilya and Petr put our Coke bottles in the river to keep them cool while we laid our towels and blankets under the embrace

174

of a large, sweeping tree. We undressed down to our bathing suits and waded into the water to watch the scene; several fishermen had set up their lines, and off in the distance a boy paddled by in a kayak.

"This is so peaceful," Rowenna said. "Standing here like this, I feel so connected—to the water flowing by, to the sand under my feet, to the people here in Kiev, and everywhere."

At that moment Ilya and Gleb came splashing into the water, breaking the mood. I tried swimming with them, but the current was very strong, and after a few minutes I gave up and returned to shore.

Then, suddenly, a scream. We all turned to see Darla hopping around on one foot by the shore and crying. She had cut her foot on a small twig in the water, and Rowenna, Petr, and Fyodor rushed over to her. "We must take her for medical help," Petr said. "There's a small first aid station near the entrance where we came in."

Fyodor picked Darla up and put her on his shoulders, and they walked off into the woods followed by Rowenna and Petr. "We'll be back shortly," Petr said. "Don't worry. It's not too serious."

It was common for beach areas to have small first aid stations. They were staffed by medical assistants rather than doctors because they normally treated less serious problems. Like all other medical treatment in the Soviet Union, it was free, and it didn't matter that Darla was a foreigner—the medical staff were pleased to treat her, too.

As we waited for their return, Betty took the softball and baseball bat Darla had brought to show the students how to play, and we pitched some balls to Ilya and Gleb. I took pictures, then wandered off down the beach to explore. A few people were perched under trees reading; a small girl floated by on a yellow raft; and a couple played a game of badminton in the wooded grove. Perhaps most fascinating were the two heavyset women doing exercises. Wearing colorful bikinis, they stood face to face about five feet apart and moved their heads from right to left in quick jerky motions; then, they dropped their heads down to their chests and quickly back up again. This cycle was repeated several times; then, with their arms stretched out, they began a routine of bending over twice on each side. They reminded me of marionettes on a string.

By the time I got back, the others had returned and were sitting on the blanket talking. Betty asked the boys about their studies and plans for the future.

"I have a girlfriend and I'm thinking about getting married while we're both still in school," Fyodor said. "We think that will help to steady us, so we can concentrate on our studies."

Gleb had different ideas. "I want to be practical and wait until I get established in a job before I get married." Similarly, Ilya wanted to wait, and it seemed one reason was that he was quite handsome and popular with the girls. "I'm enjoying my freedom right now. I like dating a number of people and probably will not settle down for at least two more years."

"Who pays on a date?" Rowenna asked.

"Most dating is Dutch," Gleb said, "because we all have about the same amount of money, which is not very much."

Betty wondered if there were alcohol or drug problems at school, but apparently this didn't seem to be prevalent.

"I don't know anyone involved in drugs," Gleb said, glancing around at the others who expressed their agreement.

"It isn't very common," Ilya added. "I have heard about people taking pills or marijuana, but not in our circles. The people we know all tend to be fairly serious students, so drugs are not something we know about."

There was time for one last swim before we had to return for lunch. We all waded back into the water; Darla hobbled alongside us, her foot wrapped in a big white bandage, and dipped her good foot in the water. Ilya and Gleb swam upstream against the current as far as they could go. When they returned, we packed up our gear and, once again, Fyodor perched Darla on his shoulders as he walked.

This time we followed a shorter path closer to the riverbank, and in just a few minutes we were on the bridge. I was in the rear taking pictures, when Gleb shouted.

"It looks like someone is about to jump!" He pointed to a man hovering on the outside of the railing, perhaps 200 feet over the river. Because I come from San Francisco where people have committed suicide jumping off the Golden Gate and other bridges, I thought this is what Gleb meant. Then I learned that jumping off this bridge was a daredevil sport in which about a dozen men had succeeded, and this one was deciding whether or not to try.

We watched for several minutes along with a small crowd that had gathered. Finally, Ilya grew impatient and commented on the late hour, so we pressed on, never knowing the outcome of the drama on the bridge.

After lunch, Boris took a few of us to the Museum of Ukrainian Art, housed in a Romanesque building that brought to mind a palace for Roman emperors. It was a fitting setting for the art, most of which featured pictures of saints and other religious figures from the Middle Ages. There were also portraits of Ukrainian nobles from a few centuries later, with long handle-bar mustaches and gilded robes. Only the paintings from the twentieth century, glorifying the peasant and the Revolution, seemed somehow out of place in this one-time home of Ukrainian nobility.

We passed a painting of women clad in filmy white dresses, placing wreathes in the river, and I mentioned to Boris that it reminded me of a similar story we had heard in Minsk. "It's an old legend told in so many places," he replied, "that perhaps it really is true."

Afterwards, he took us to a Ukrainian souvenir shop with traditionally crafted items. There were dresses with intricate lacing and stitching, wooden boxes with the distinctive circles and cross-hatching of the Carpathian mountain villages, and plaques with dancing figures in ancient folk costumes. The work was exquisite and expensive: I looked at one dress that cost 300 rubles ($500), surprised to find something so costly in a local rubles store.

"Local people will save for these items," Boris explained. "They are special because they are part of our heritage." He suggested we not buy here, however. "You will find similar merchandise in the foreign currency stores at much lower prices."

Boris asked if we would like some ice cream, and when everyone said yes at once, he took us to a small ice cream and coffee shop. There were about twenty people in line for ice cream (there was a second line for coffee), and I supposed it would move quickly. However, after ten minutes we had hardly moved, and Boris suggested that the rest of us sit down.

Finally, after half an hour, Boris arrived at the head of the line. Curious about why it took so long, I went up and discovered that the woman was using an ordinary spoon, not a scoop, and then weighing each portion to assure the exact amount. If the portion was over, she would carefully scoop out the excess, and if under, add a bit more. It seemed an odd economy, given the waiting crowds. "Oh, well, we get used to this waiting," Boris said.

Next we headed for the foreign currency store. Luci left to meet Jennifer for a dinner date with three of the Soviets we had met, and Boris directed her to a hotel where she could pick up a bottle of vodka at a much lower price than the Soviets had to pay in their own state liquor stores.

On the way to the bus we passed a woman in a white lab coat weighing people on the street, and Boris commented that this was usually how people weighed themselves. "It costs only two kopeks. I don't know anyone who owns their own scale; very few stores sell them, and they are quite expensive."

While on the bus, I noticed several people darting across the street, and asked Boris if they had penalties for jaywalking.

He said it is considered a minor offense, and if a policeman notices, he can write a ticket and the fine of three rubles must be paid on the spot. If the person says he has no money, he many need to show some identification so the state can collect from his wages later.

I expressed surprise at this process of paying the officer. "In the U.S., we might consider that bribery," and I explained how people mailed in their fines or went to court to protest.

"In these small matters, we consider it much easier to pay the ticket directly. The fine is so low, I doubt if there would ever be an appeal. People may complain, but they pay. If someone is caught doing it again, he pays exactly the same amount—the fine in such matters is fixed."

An older woman boarded the bus with some heavy packages, and almost immediately, a man seated near the entrance got up and nodded to her to take his seat. Such courteous behavior seemed to be common practice, and Boris told us it was generally accepted for people to get up for anyone who was old or weak.

In Kiev and other Ukrainian cities, the *beryozka*, a name that means "birch tree," is called a Kashtan store, meaning "chestnut tree." This one occupied the lower floor in an apartment complex. There were several aisles of Ukraine specialties, plus shelves in back for the more usual items—appliances, fur hats, jewelry, vodka, and various foodstuffs. As I stood admiring some colorful wooden eggs painted in bright-red and black floral patterns, Boris urged me away.

"Those are just for tourists," he said. "They're made dozens at a time at the factory. These others are the real, traditional ones," and he pointed to a basket of smaller, more intricately painted eggs in muted brown and purple tones wrapped in a delicate webbing of lace. Pointing to rows of wooden boxes with variegated cross-hatch patterns, he added, "Many things look traditional, but they're really not. You have to know what is authentic and what isn't."

I purchased the delicate, muted eggs, and we returned to the hotel. Boris promised to pick us up at eight o'clock for an evening at Alyosha and Anya's.

When he arrived with Ilya, Petr, and Petr's girlfriend, Valya, there were eleven of us waiting for them. Anya and Alyosha lived on a quiet, tree-lined street near the right bank of the river. As we passed into a narrow alley between two buildings, we suddenly saw them waving and dangling out of a fourth-floor window. Inside, we met Alyosha's father, Victor, who lived with them and expressed sincere pleasure at being a part of this happy occasion.

They had set up a long table which took up the bulk of the room. It was covered with a lacy white linen tablecloth and was brimming with goodies—tea, cookies, and all sorts of cakes including chocolate, cheesecake, and white cake—all homemade. On either side, they had pushed up beds covered with green throws to create two long couches.

As we spread out around the table, Boris once again began the gathering with a small welcoming speech, followed by Anya and Valya serving the cakes. Boris announced that he was collecting American sayings and asked if we could suggest some for his collection, so we offered a few: Life is just a bowl of cherries . . . A stitch in time saves nine . . . If the shoe fits, wear it . . . A fool and his money are soon parted . . . Easy come, easy go . . . What goes around, comes around . . . Par for the course.

Boris rapidly scribbled our suggestions in a notebook, occasionally asking the meaning.

"What about some Russian or Ukrainian expressions?" I suggested, so Boris read us a few from his list. These turned out to be somewhat more abstract and philosophical than ours, and perhaps more tied to an agricultural heritage.

" 'Seven do not wait for me . . . Time and tide wait for no one.' " We had never heard these and looked perplexed, so he explained, "They mean that everything has its own pace and life goes on, so do not expect it to wait for you."

Boris tried another. "If someone says something stupid, or not what you are expecting, you answer, 'Hello, I am your aunt.' " Again we looked puzzled. "It's about meeting a dumb or unexpected response with one that's equally so."

He decided to return to the more common sayings. " 'The devil himself would break his leg.' This means it's a very diffi-cult situation for anyone. 'Measure seven times before cutting one' . . . 'Think seven times before making a step.' That's sim-ilar to your 'Look before you leap.' 'One fisherman sees another from a great distance.' This means one person can recognize another of like background when he sees him."

"Like 'Birds of a feather flock together,' " we all chimed in.

Boris nodded and continued. " 'We meet people by their clothes and see them off by their brain.' When we see someone we don't know, we judge them by their clothes or outer self. But as we get closer to people, we judge them by their deeper self. In other words, don't judge people prematurely." It was intri-guing discovering that Soviets and Americans had sayings with similar meanings, just different images, and the discussion helped us feel closer together.

Boris flipped a few more pages. "Now here's the last one," he said. " 'If God gives it to you, He will take it from you.' " We were a little surprised to hear Boris use "God," since we thought most people in the Soviet Union were conditioned not to. "This is a traditional saying," he explained, "and goes back many generations. It mainly cautions against counting on things, since bad fortune alternates with the good."

Boris wanted to finish by telling us a Russian joke. "What are the six paradoxes of Soviet society? They are: 1) We don't have unemployment, but nobody really works. 2) Nobody works, but everybody gets his salary. 3) Everybody gets his salary, but there is nothing to buy. 4) There is nothing to buy, but there is everything in everybody's home. 5) There is everything in everybody's home, but people are not satisfied. 6) People are not satisfied, but everybody votes for the candidate."

We all laughed, and Boris said there were many jokes like that. "People enjoy mocking the establishment or aspects of society that don't work. It's a way of lightening up some of the heavy burdens we share."

While we were sharing sayings and jokes, others were trading stories about home, family, work, and everyday life. Anya and Valya brought out more cheesecakes and a large bowl of cherries, and Alyosha and his father, a quiet, thin man who worked as an engineer, led everyone in a series of toasts.

When it was time to leave, Anya handed me a small white gift box which contained a black box with pictures of cherries.

"It's a Ukrainian souvenir."

I gave her some *glasnost* buttons for herself and others in the club, and she put one on a bulletin board with perhaps one hundred other buttons. "It's very popular to collect them," she said by way of explanation. "When we go someplace or meet someone, we get a button as a souvenir."

Gert thought that since Boris had welcomed us in English, it would be appropriate to say our goodbyes in Russian. We clustered together in the hall and sang the song she had taught us: "May there always be sunshine . . . may there always be peace."

━━━━━━━━━

That night we had a feeling of completion. We were getting ready to leave not only Kiev but the Soviet Union, and as we reflected on the evening we agreed it had been one of the high points of the trip, a kind of summation. Angela expressed it well: "This evening, this entire time in Kiev, everyone has really gone out for us. I feel so nurtured, like a royal guest. The first party they had for us, all the places they took us, our gathering tonight, seeing us home as they always do—they have all gone out of their way to take care of us. They may not have as much as we do in material terms, but we have been given something much more precious."

It was a heartening conclusion to our journey. Tomorrow we would be leaving Kiev—and heading home.

PART VII

GOING HOME

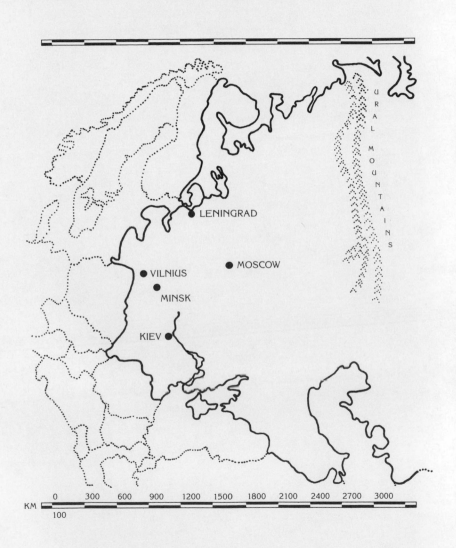

CHAPTER 18

The Last Day and Beginning Our Return

Going home. It was hard to believe our trip was almost over and that most of us would never again see these people who had become our friends. Our last day in Kiev passed in a series of snapshot-like impressions.

Our morning meeting began on a somewhat somber note as Betty spoke about plans for our departure and asked us to have everything ready by five o'clock. We would be taking the six-thirty overnight train to Moscow; we had the tickets at long last.

Some people had plans to get together with the Soviets one last time, while others wanted to do some shopping. Nalya offered to take a group of us to a special Social Photography Exhibit.

"It's a real first for the Ukraine and the Soviet Union. In the past, such an exhibit wasn't allowed because it would have been considered too critical of Soviet society, even viewed as anti-Soviet propaganda. Basically it shows everyday life—the bad as well as the good. That it can now be shown is an historical occasion."

We took the metro downtown and once again experienced the hustle of the city. Only the city market, held in a high-domed building and having the atmosphere of an oversized county fair, seemed somehow removed from the fast pace.

At first glance, the photo exhibit looked ordinary and many of the photographs even seemed crudely taken. But it was not the technical competence of the photographers which characterized the importance of this show; rather, it represented an expression of the spirit of *glasnost*.

There were bold and eloquent studies: Peasant scenes from the countryside, fat bureaucrats, a middle-aged woman making a last stab at catching a man, a worker sleeping under a sign encouraging productivity, protest marchers carrying signs for saving the forests. One of the signs read: Thanks to Gorbachev, People Have the Opportunity to Make Demands.

The show presented a revealing look at a society in the throes of change.

Our group went briefly to St. Vladimir's, an old church at the edge of the city. Inside, women lit prayer candles and clustered around two priests who were leading the services. From time to time, someone would hand the priests a small slip of paper with their own names or those of others, and the priests would recite prayers for them. Later, they could pick up these pieces of paper, which were now blessed, and keep them as talismans.

On the way back, I stood in the metro plaza near our hotel taking pictures, using my long-distance lens to zoom in on people getting on the bus or making purchases in the market. Ironically, just as I was thinking how easy it was to get these candid photos, much like the photographers at the exhibit, a police officer approached me. He pointed to my camera, saying, "Nyet" and "Close it up." This was my first police encounter of the trip, despite the many cautions people had given me before I left about taking pictures, particularly in places like train stations and the metro. For a moment a sudden fear passed over me. Would he take my film or my camera? I floundered around in my camera case trying to find my lens cap, feeling that the sooner I closed it up, the sooner I could placate this officer who might even have visions of my being some kind of a spy. Finally I found my lens cap and put it on.

"*Spasibo*," he said, meaning "thank you," and moved on.

I felt a rush of relief and hurried from the station. Apparently he realized I was just a tourist and wanted me to put away my camera to prevent any intrusion on people's privacy. Safely away from the metro and the police officer, I quickly finished up my roll of film near our hotel and went in for lunch. Afterward, Nalya arrived and I asked her about the incident.

"I'm sure your taking photographs in the metro was fine. Before the changes in the law it might not have been, but much more is allowed now—except taking photos of airports and anything associated with the military. Because there is still confusion over what is allowed and what isn't, people sometimes think that photographs are not allowed, when in fact there is no law against it. Perhaps this is what your officer thought.

"Often it is only necessary to check with people higher up to know whether there is permission. Of course, you may not be able to do this with a policeman, even if he is wrong. But with others, do not let that first 'no' put you off."

About a half dozen of the students had arrived by now, including Boris, Ilya, Petr, and Valya, ready to help us to the train. They loaded our luggage on the bus and clambered aboard with us, found porters at the station, and walked us to the waiting train.

In a few minutes our luggage was loaded and it was time for goodbyes. Angela presented a backpack to Ilya that she had purchased at the foreign currency store: "For your mountain climbing and for doing so much to help us." Rowenna had some children's books for Nalya's group, and the rest of us had posters, buttons, and other small gifts to give. I promised to send a *Glasnost* game to the group as soon as it was published, and Nalya said she would send me pictures of people playing it. I told Boris I would send him a book of American sayings for his collection. "Just don't send them by post," he said good-naturedly.

As the train pulled out of the station, we all squeezed beside the door or hung out of compartment windows waving goodbye.

Our last glimpse was of everyone standing on the platform blowing kisses and waving, much like our saying goodbye in Moscow. But this felt even sadder because we had spent almost two solid days with these people. We had come to know and love them.

Back in our compartment, Jennifer brushed away a few last tears. "I was just thinking about leaving the people we've become so close to. It's like leaving our family, and leaving a little of ourselves behind."

CHAPTER 19

What Can We Learn
from Each Other?

Our last day in the Soviet Union was a changing kaleidoscope
of trains, buses, hotels, and planes. It felt good to be back under
the protective wing of the Intourist guides who looked after us
and made sure we made all of our connections.

We arrived in Moscow around six-thirty in the morning,
and our new guide, Lydia, a trim, dark-haired woman of about
forty with an efficient, well-organized executive aura about her,
shepherded us onto our waiting bus and explained the plan for
the day. We would go to an Intourist hotel for breakfast and
head for the airport at three.

After breakfast we gathered to say goodbye to Susan and
Charles, who were going off on their own for an extended stay
in the Soviet Union, then fanned out for the day. A few people
went to see an exhibition of Russian icons, frescoes, and paintings from all over the Soviet Union, others took a boat trip on
the Moscow River, and some went to the *beryozka* to buy last-
minute souvenirs.

I took the metro downtown to the San Francisco-Moscow
Teleport Office to leave a letter of authorization for Gennady;
he needed it to act on my behalf in trying to find a producer for
my game. The whole process took much longer than I expected,
and I would arrive back just in time to make our bus.

The primary delay was due to the lack of higher technology.

At the time of my visit, word processors, fax machines, public typewriters, and copy machines were not yet available, so I had to write my letter in longhand and deliver it personally to this office if I wanted to ensure Gennady's receiving it. The process felt incredibly slow and made me aware of how fortunate we are in the U.S. to have the latest innovations at our disposal—what ended up taking three hours I could have faxed, dictated into an answering machine, or copied and deposited in the mail in a matter of minutes.

Still, while the delay made me impatient and frustrated, my other experiences served to remind me of some old-fashioned values often eclipsed in the name of progress. For example, I will never forget the man in the metro who so beautifully exemplified honesty, a characteristic Soviet people hold in high regard. I was at a change machine when this man tapped me on the shoulder and pointed to a ruble on the floor. Although I didn't understand the words, he was clearly asking me if I had dropped it. I said no and started toward the turnstile, but happened to look back and see him approach another person, then finally pick up the ruble and take it to a nearby guard. For some reason, this simple display of good faith touched me deeply. It was almost of another era, still lingering on here.

Another incident occurred when I had to find my way back in a hurry through a maze of six metro lines all coming together in one station. I managed to get on the train, but still wasn't sure if I was on the right line when, suddenly, I found myself in the middle of a group of people determined to help me understand, despite the language barrier, that it was the right line but I needed to change trains. When the train stopped, a woman gestured for me to follow her out the doors, then, still using gestures, indicated that I should wait. She waited with me, and when the right train came along, she motioned for me to get on.

When I tried to give her some buttons as a way of saying thank you, she said, "No, no," and, smiling broadly, indicated that I must hurry. I realized that for her to take something in return would interfere with the pure altruism of her action. I could see by the map that I was on the right train and sighed with relief. I had to be back in twenty minutes to meet our bus, and now I knew I would make it. I surely would have ended up in the wrong place if it hadn't been for the concern of the people on that metro car.

It was a nice image to leave with, and I wondered what it might be like for a stranger in the U.S. who didn't speak English. Would people help? I hoped they would.

Everyone was strangely quiet as we rode to the airport, reflecting on the experiences we had had, on the meaning of our journey. When we arrived at the airport, Kurt, Angela, and I still had rubles to change; it's illegal to take them out of the country. Lydia pointed us in the direction of the bank, and we got in a line of about two dozen people. Time passed, and we glanced nervously at our watches.

"I'll go check with the others," Kurt said. He returned to announce that they were still waiting to get through customs.

"Well, maybe it's apropos that we should spend our last minutes in Moscow in line," Angela joked.

We finally reached the window, only to discover that we were in the wrong line! The clerk pointed us toward the bank a few doors down, where fortunately only a few people were waiting, and we quickly transacted our business. Our mistake in choosing the longer, slower line served as a final reminder of misperceptions that are so easy to make.

A short time later we were through customs and Passport Control and on the plane. I had a feeling of being finished—no more notes, no more picture taking, no more being constantly "on"—observing everything, asking questions.

But not quite. Now while we were still together, Betty wanted to have one last get-together to discuss what the trip had meant to us. As she put it, "This trip is not just a journey to the Soviet Union. It's also a journey into yourselves."

In Helsinki, we gathered in Betty's room, and each in turn described what had most impressed him or her about the trip. In sharing, we were building a kind of circle, a network of interlocking connections tying us to each other, to the people we had met, and to those with whom we had yet to share our experiences. We all expressed appreciation for each group member's unique contribution to the whole, then imparted a special memory we would be bringing home.

Angela began. "Maybe it's easier to take the time to get to know others more intimately in a foreign country. I find that at home I get caught up in my routine and don't have time for my friends, or social issues. I was most impressed with the time people here spent with us—people who might never see us again. This is a powerful message for me about caring and connecting. I want to bring that message back to my own hometown and spend more time with the people I know there."

Bill admired the basic honesty of the people. "I felt that if I left my possessions someplace, I could expect to see them when I got back. Boris said something interesting about the way Soviet children are brought up: 'Early in life we are told by our parents we must maintain our character and not be ashamed by what we do.' I think the emphasis on community also encourages this integrity; they tend to stay in one place more than we do and have less immigration. I get the feeling they watch out for each other more."

Charity appreciated the people's courage despite many hardships, and cited the war memorial at Khatyn in Belorussia as one of the more moving experiences of her life.

Others were impressed by the warmth and friendship of the Soviet people and by how safe and secure we felt wherever we went. "To me, the key to the trip was meeting the people," Carolyn said. "The close friendships and memories we have made will be with us throughout our lives."

Like Angela, Rowenna felt a need to bring what we had learned back to our own communities. "We have seen a great deal of compassion in the people we have met, and I want to translate that into my friendships at home. I want to encourage others to be citizen diplomats, too."

Jennifer felt a need to temper the appreciation with a recognition of the problems Soviets still faced. "We have seen so much good, in many ways, the best side of the Soviet Union. We have met with the intelligentsia, and people who are thoughtful and aware. It's an excellent counterbalance to the kinds of negative images so many of us have grown up with and that so many people in the U.S. still have. Yet, at the same time, I don't want to look only through rose-colored glasses.

"There are areas of their society that the people don't like, just as there are aspects to ours which are a problem. Perhaps the key to creating a better world lies in taking a closer look at what doesn't work, and in finding ways to contribute solutions to each other's problems, if possible."

Her words struck a deep chord in all of us. There are positives and negatives on both sides, and some very basic differences from which we all can learn a great deal. For example, based on our different histories, Americans and Soviets have very different concepts of "rights" and "freedoms." Our background is one of independence, personal initiative, and entrepreneurial spirit. We still nurture memories of the lawless frontier, and honor the bold and innovative. What is important to Americans are freedoms "to" have such human rights as free speech, free press, and the rights to bear arms and to protest.

The Soviets, too, consider their rights important: the right to a job, to housing, to free education, medical and child care. Because they come from a background of strong central control, they value their freedoms "from" such social problems and concerns as a high crime rate or a growing homeless population.

So much springs from, and begins with, these basic assumptions and understandings about how things are and what is right. Perhaps by looking more at our own and others' assumptions and meanings we can learn much and also teach each other. The American value of *individual initiative*, for example, has helped us create a highly developed technological society that frees us to create, experience, and enjoy more of life. By contrast, the Soviets value *cooperation* so highly because they view it as a way to make sure everyone in their country is fed, clothed, employed, and taken care of. Yet combining these two values might help to create a better social balance.

As we spoke of these differences, we realized that attitudes on both sides were changing—truly, a door was opening between us. Betty pointed out that some Soviets were starting to think of freedom in our terms, and many Americans were beginning to appreciate the heart of the Soviets, their propensity for caring and nurturing.

"We're learning to see each other's freedoms as supplementary to our own. For instance, a father we met on the train to Moscow said he hoped his sons would gain the 'freedoms to' that Americans have—to travel, to speak openly, to have privacy. 'It's too late for me,' he said, 'but I want this for them.' And younger Soviets are starting to request these freedoms. Only in the past year have they been able to protest, and one freedom they openly request is to be able to travel out of the country." Again, these early stirrings were to prove to be prophetic, for Soviets have gained these freedoms now.

Betty continued. "Certainly there is a lot to be said for the 'freedoms from' which the Soviets have. While they may want to supplement their way of life with some of our freedoms, this doesn't mean they want to trade places with us. They like their security and the feeling of protection they have, and they tend to see the U.S. with all its freedoms as one vast, competitive jungle; this is not what they want. In fact, many Soviet emigres have had trouble adjusting in America because they don't feel protected. We value our individual freedoms, yet have sacrificed much as a result of our emphasis on them. Perhaps the events taking place in our world are a way of finding a kind of global balance."

"I think freedom is a state of mind," Jennifer said. "Some Soviets felt very free to come with us into the hotel, while others didn't. It seems old images and ideas die hard, not only for us about the Soviets, but for the Soviets about themselves."

"Yes," Betty agreed. "It's interesting how powerful images

can be. Sometimes doormen *do* stop Soviets and check their passports, but Irina sails through easily. She says she simply puts on her 'American woman face,' looks straight ahead, walks briskly, and is not afraid. Those who don't feel confident are the ones who get stopped."

Charity confessed that she had felt intimidated on a couple of occasions by some officials we had encountered, and wasn't sure if this was her own misperception or if they, indeed, might have felt stuck in some minor position and needed to display their power as a way to feel more important.

The conversation turned to images of the Soviet state and rights of privacy. Angela wondered about how much we might have been observed, if at all. "Here we were meeting with Soviets, even bringing them equipment such as cameras and answering machines. Even though *we* know our intentions are good, was anyone concerned? I can imagine how this might be of interest to the FBI if it were happening in the U.S."

"The only time I felt watched was when a camera crew was filming the festival and the protest in Vilnius," Kurt said.

"It's another area where we have many preconceptions," Betty suggested. "Even the Soviets joke about this idea of being watched. When we were guests at Alyosha's, several flies were buzzing around. Petr killed a few, but one was insistent. Petr said, 'Oh, that's a KGB agent.'

"Another time I was with Nalya, trying to call Moscow. For an hour we kept getting a busy signal, and when we finally got through, the line went dead, though it ended up coming back on. Nalya said, 'Oh, they were probably changing the tape.' The point is we have all these images, and we don't know what the reality may be."

"It's like comparing the public and private faces of people," Rowenna said. "On the outside, dealing with foreigners or with the public, Soviets may seem overly official, maybe even cold at times, as Charity was feeling. But in fact, I have been impressed with the way people here seem to have warmer, closer friendships than we do in the U.S. Boris said he could invite anyone he wanted to Alyosha's apartment for dinner because he knew him so well, and knew Alyosha liked to have American guests. That shows a really strong friendship."

There had been some occasional snags, but the warmth and generosity of the people stood out above all. Betty ended the meeting with the hope that we would remember this feeling of appreciation we had for the Soviets, and that we would be inspired to carry it even further.

Now it was time simply to relax. I found my way to the sauna and pool for a long, relaxing swim.

In the morning we had our last meeting as a group, and this time we crowded in Betty and Kurt's room with cameras to take group photos.

"Now we need to get ready for reentry," Betty began. "As we go back into our everyday lives again, we may tend to discount the intensity of our experience. You may find that you have changed, perhaps in very subtle ways, and since others haven't shared the experience and may not understand or want to hear all the details you're eager to give them, it's important to know that we are all just a phone call away. This group can continue to be your support group.

"It's something like having gone off and fallen in love; you have a lot you want to say about that person, but others are not very interested, which you may find hard to understand. We have had a love affair with the Soviet Union, but other people may have hostile, negative feelings, even thinking of the Soviet Union as an enemy, and they may not want to hear your glowing reports. Despite the changes happening to transform the system, they still may not want to accept how free you felt to wander around on your own and how warm and friendly the people are, or else they may want to focus on the shortcomings of the Soviet system.

"So it's best to just present your own experience. Go slowly, a little at a time. Point out both sides of the Soviet equation—the bitter and the sweet. Share what you've discovered, in yourself and in the people you have met. Tell them what a citizen diplomacy trip is all about—developing understanding, building connections, working for change through person-to-person contact. Clearing out false images and superficial impressions is part of the goal, as is finding areas in which we can work together for a better tomorrow."

On the plane going home, I thought about this vision of working together for change, and I realized that each one of us could make our own contribution.

It was in this spirit that I decided to write this book. By sharing what I have experienced, I hope that others might be inspired to be part of this changemakers process that is reshaping our world today. Through our efforts perhaps we can contribute to making the world now emerging one of freedom, peace, and prosperity, based on greater mutual understanding, respect, and trust.

CHAPTER 20

Preparing for a Citizen
Diplomacy Trip

If you are interested in becoming a citizen diplomat and traveling to the Soviet Union or to other countries, here are some suggestions on how to do it.

Probably the best way is to go on a citizen diplomacy trip sponsored by an organization, as I did. The advantages here are that you will be going with a group of like-minded people and traveling with a leader who will have contacts in the cities you are visiting. The organization helps with advance preparation by supplying a recommended reading list and articles that will give you an updated, in-depth understanding of current topics, places you will be visiting, and people you will meet. This will aid you in asking thoughtful, intelligent questions and will provide a basis for building a rapport. The organizations may also help with an advance primer including tapes on learning the language.

A second way to get involved in citizen diplomacy is by offering to be a host or contact for people who come to the U.S. This is a good way to further understanding among nations and deepen the ties of friendship.

Third, if you are going on a trip with a group for another purpose, such as a study trip or special-interest tour, you can always supplement it with one-on-one citizen diplomacy to develop more personal relationships with the people you encounter.

Finally, you can incorporate citizen diplomacy when traveling on your own to deepen your connections with people, promote understanding, and create personal ties that may continue to grow in the future.

Some Tips for Becoming a Citizen Diplomat When You Travel

1. Learn as much as you can about the country you will visit through books, articles, films, lectures, etc. The more you know, the better your experience will be, and the process of learning is a fascinating journey in itself.

In particular, it is helpful to have information on the following topics:

- geography and history
- cultural norms and values
- government structure and current political situation
- religious beliefs
- educational system
- the roles of men and women
- everyday life and routine
- transportation systems
- accepted dress and modes of conduct
- cost of, and kinds of merchandise available
- types of gifts appreciated

2. Learn and follow the rules of the country you are visiting. Consider yourself a guest in the country; you don't want to do anything to offend your host. For example, in the Soviet Union, don't engage in black market dealing. Charles, one of our group who was approached, dealt with this situation by saying: "I don't want to exchange money but I will exchange ideas." The black marketeer was amazed that Charles wanted to know more about him and his way of life, saying he assumed Americans weren't interested because the ones he had met

seemed to know so little. Their street encounter ended up as a spirited conversation and the beginning of a friendship.

3. How you dress and act is important, especially if you are traveling in a country where people generally have lower incomes and don't spend a great deal of money on clothing. Dressing too upscale can create barriers to communication.

For example, we were advised to dress modestly and conservatively. The Center suggested skirts, slacks, blouses, and sweaters for women, and shirts without ties, jeans or slacks for men, a casual everyday look. It's also wise to be apprised of weather conditions, bring appropriate outer wear and comfortable walking shoes, and a more formal dress or suit for the theater or official meetings.

We were also asked to be aware of the formal, polite way Soviets treat each other, in contrast to the more casual manners of Americans. Soviets are very warm and hospitable, but also more restrained.

4. Be open to looking at the world from the point of view of the people you are visiting, rather than in terms of your own beliefs, values, standards, and expectations. Recognize there are many valid ways of looking at the world, and be open to developing a broader perspective.

5. Communicate with people so that they feel comfortable. For example, ask questions in a neutral way so that people aren't exposed to your prejudices or feel that you are grilling them. Learn to listen, showing you really do want to understand. Apprise yourself of any and all sensitive issues people might wish to avoid, and then either be very careful when touching upon these areas or avoid them altogether.

6. Be receptive and understanding when people make comments or ask questions about your own country that suggest wrong information or negative stereotypes. Don't become angry, but gently correct these misconceptions. On the other hand, if people point out negative information that is true, such as the American homeless or drug problems, you might simply acknowledge the situation, explain it, or put it in context.

7. Learn the language. At least be able to read street signs and get around, and try to learn common expressions so that you have some ability to ask questions, order food, shop, say "thank you," etc.

8. Be ready to talk to people wherever you are and look for ways to start conversations: Make a friendly comment to someone, offer a souvenir, compliment parents on their child.

9. Be respectful if you are taking photographs. Don't just snap away, unless you are in a very public place where picture taking is generally accepted. Asking people for permission is an excellent way to open a conversation, and you might consider taking a Polaroid camera in order to give them their pictures instantly. It is in the spirit of citizen diplomacy to offer something in exchange for a photo. If taking photos of children, for example, you might give them gum, candy, or friendship pins.

10. Be ready and willing to venture off the beaten tourist track. Go to the produce market at seven in the morning; visit a public bath or a courtroom; shop in a local department store or eat at a neighborhood restaurant. The creative opportunities are innumerable.

11. Collect names of people who live in the area you plan to visit. If you have time, write in advance or call a few days ahead to let them know you are coming. Calling and making arrangements to get together after you arrive is fine, but you run the risk of a missed connection. If it's your first meeting, plan to start off with something casual, like coffee, or you can meet on the street or in front of your hotel. You might invite your contacts to join you and your group for a meal or on an outing.

12. If the people you meet are willing to meet other citizen diplomats coming to their country, take their names and share this information either during your trip or after you return. Our group kept track of receptive contacts by writing their names in the "Worrier of the Day" book.

13. Bring along small gifts for conversation openers when you encounter people on the streets and for Intourist guides, bus drivers, and hotel staff. You can use buttons, bookmarks,

postcards, greeting cards, and similar items to give away as souvenirs.

14. Bring along special gifts to exchange with people who become your friends or do something especially thoughtful, such as inviting you to their home for dinner or taking time to show you or your group around. It helps to find out in advance what people might like or need.

Here is a list of suggestions: paperback books, magazines, artwork, business-card holders, posters, costume jewelry, pins, perfumes, cosmetics, pantyhose, scarves, pens, records or cassette tapes, blank tapes, solar calculators, photos, and items for children such as coloring books and crayons, children's books, Yoyos, and Frisbees.

In choosing gifts, be sensitive to the tastes of your hosts. For example, Soviets consider publications such as *Playboy* or *Cosmopolitan*, pornography. Similarly, we were advised not to bring books which they feel cast an unfavorable light on their country, such as Hedrick Smith's *The Russians*. It was fine to bring our own Bible or religious material, but not numerous copies, which might look as if we were there to proselytize or, worse, sell on the black market. You don't want to incur the wrath of and perhaps confiscation by customs agents by bringing in anything inappropriate.

However, it's okay to bring in several articles or mechanical items as gifts. For example, on our trip Betty brought a number of gifts she had promised to Soviets on previous trips, including a used answering machine for a man trying to set up a small publishing cooperative. In the Soviet Union, an answering machine would have cost close to $500, if available at all; this one, valued at $50 and donated, was perfect for his needs. When I asked Betty if it was legal to bring in so much, wondering if customs might think we were dealing in the black market, she assured me it was perfectly all right as long as they were gifts.

15. Know what to bring with you and what to leave at home. We were warned against bringing in anything that needed batteries, because they are hard to get. Similarly, we were ad-

vised not to bring too much luggage because travel within the Soviet Union allows only up to forty-four pounds, including all carry-on luggage *and* purses. Items we might want to take included toilet paper, a scarce commodity in the Soviet Union and of a much rougher quality.

16. Follow up as promised after you return home. If you have told someone you would write, or send certain items, do so. Aside from being a common courtesy, your follow-through helps the people you have met feel more receptive to meeting others in the future.

17. When you return, think of ways to share your experience with others. Put together a little presentation book of your trip, create a slide show, or give talks to local groups.

These ideas are designed to help you get started in citizen diplomacy. In the Appendix following, you will find a list of organizations which conduct citizen diplomacy trips or are otherwise involved in working toward improving Soviet-American relations. Some are involved in promoting citizen diplomacy and a more peaceful world generally.

If you take a trip to the U.S.S.R. or any other country, I hope these ideas will prove useful and help to create an even more exciting, fulfilling trip. Or, if you continue to remain an armchair traveler, you can always discuss what you learn on your "travels" with others. We all can be bridges to peace, in our own ways.

APPENDIX

Organizations Working to Bridge the Barriers

The following organizations are involved in working to further Soviet-American relationships, arrange trips to the U.S.S.R., or both. You can write to them for further information. This is not intended to be an exhaustive list, since there is a huge and growing list of organizations involved in this field. I have listed some of the main ones that I have heard about. My thanks, too, to the Institute of Soviet-American Relations, which publishes *Surviving Together*. This has been a major source for listings of many of these organizations.

Anniversary Tours, 330 Seventh Avenue, Suite 1700, New York, NY 10001. (212) 465-1200.

Center for U.S.-U.S.S.R. Initiatives, 3268 Sacramento Street, San Francisco, CA 94115. (415) 346-1875.

Citizen Exchange Council, 12 West 31st Street, New York, NY 10001. (212) 643-1985.

Diomedes, Inc., 3105 Washington Street, San Francisco, CA 94115. (415) 563-4731.

General Tours, 770 Broadway, New York, NY 10003. (212) 598-1800.

International Peace Walk, P.O. Box 2958, San Rafael, CA 94912. (415) 453-0792.

Peace Cruise, P.O. Box 5103, Woodmont, CT 06460. (203) 878-4769.

Peace Links, 747 Eighth Street, SE, Washington, D.C. 20003. (202) 544-0805.

Pioneer Travel, 203 Allston Street, Cambridge, MA 02139. (617) 648-2020.

Professional Seminar Consultants, 3194 Lawson Blvd., Oceanside, NY 11572.

Russart Travel Agency, 291 Geary Street, San Francisco, CA 94102. (415) 781-6655.

Tour Designs, Inc. 510 H Street, SW, Washington, D.C. 20024. (202) 554-5820; (800) 432-8687.

Other Organizations Working Toward Furthering Soviet-American Relations

American Committee on U.S.-Soviet Relations, 109 11th Street, SE, Washington, D.C. 20003.

Better World Society, 1140 Connecticut Avenue, NW, Washington, D.C. 20005.

Beyond War, 222 High Street, Palo Alto, CA 94301. (415) 328-7756. National organization working toward peace.

Changemakers, 308 Spruce Street, San Francisco, CA 94118. (415) 567-2747. Does slide presentations on travel in the Soviet Union.

Children as Peacemakers, 950 Battery Street, 2nd Floor, San Francisco, CA 94111. (415) 981-0916. Takes delegations of American children to the Soviet Union.

Citizens Network for Common Security, Anabel Taylor Hall, Cornell University, Ithaca, NY 14853. (607) 255-8276 or 255-8270. Tapes available on citizen diplomacy.

Institute for Soviet-American Relations, 1608 New Hampshire Avenue, N.W., Washington, D.C. 20009. (202) 387-3034. Publishes *Surviving Together*, a journal on events, activities, and organizations in the field of Soviet-American relations.

Institute for Global Communications, 3228 Sacramento Street, San Francisco, CA 94115. (415) 923-0900. Has a computer network of more than 2400 organizations involved in peace, disarmament, environmental protection, and human rights.

Institute of Noetic Sciences, P.O. Box 909, Sausalito, CA 94966. (415) 331-5650. Research and occasional trips to the U.S.S.R. in addition to other activities related to peace and developing human consciousness.

International Foundation for the Survival and Development of Humanity, 3228 Sacramento Street, San Francisco, CA 94115. (415) 776-2600.

National Council of American-Soviet Friendship, 85 East 4th Street, New York, NY 10003. (212) 254-6606. Sponsors various educational and cultural activities. Chapters around the U.S.

Peace Child Foundation, 3220 Sacramento Street, San Francisco, CA 94115. (415) 931-2593. Organizes international projects in the performing arts.

Project RAFT (Russians and Americans for Teamwork), 51 Carisa Court, Walnut Creek, CA 94596. (415) 935-4528. Leads river rafting expeditions for young people in the Soviet Union and the U.S.

San Francisco/Moscow Teleport, 3278 Sacramento Street, San Francisco, CA 94115. (415) 931-8500. Offers a communication service between the U.S. and Soviet Union.

The Center for Democracy, 358 W. 30th Street, #1A, New York, NY 10001. (212) 967-2027. Publishes the English translation of *Glasnost* magazine, originally published in the U.S.S.R.

The Foundation for Social Innovations, 3220 Sacramento Street, San Francisco, CA 94115. (415) 931-2593. Promotes innovative projects within the Soviet Union and seeks U.S. support for these activities.

US Information Moscow, 3101 Washington Street, San Francisco, CA 94115. (415) 922-2422. Publishes a comprehensive guide to East-West trade and travel, and consulting services to individuals and businesses.

US/USSR Bridges for Peace, Box 710, Norwich, VT 05055. (802) 649-1000.

Washington Research Institute, 3220 Sacramento Street, San Francisco, CA 94115. (415) 931-2593. Sponsors many Soviet-American activities; home for many groups involved in working toward improved Soviet-American relations. Also sets up U.S -Soviet communication links.

World Without War, 2929 NE Blakeley Street, Seattle, WA 98105.

About The Author

Nationally known author Gini Graham Scott, Ph.D., has published over twenty books on diverse subjects, including books on creativity, problem solving, conflict resolution, group dynamics, and travel. Her interest in the Soviet Union derives from her own background—half Ukrainian and Bulgarian through her grandparents who emigrated in the early 1900s—and her three recent trips to the Soviet Union.

She is also the creator of the exciting new game *Glasnost: The Game of Soviet-American Peace and Diplomacy*, now in stores nationwide. The game won a 1989 International Clio Award for packaging design, and it has recently been published in French and German editions for sale in France, Germany, Switzerland, Belgium, and Austria. A Russian edition is in the works. Gini Scott's photographs of the Soviet Union have also been featured in a recently released *Glasnost* calendar for 1991.

She is the founder and president of Creative Communications & Research and Changemakers. Ms. Scott has received extensive media exposure, including appearances on such shows as "Phil Donahue." She will receive her J.D. degree from the University of San Francisco in 1990. Her Ph.D. in Sociology is from the University of California at Berkeley.

Gini Graham Scott is available for speaking, workshop/seminars, and slide presentations on her travels in the Soviet

Union. She also is a business and organizational consultant, specializing in the areas of creativity, problem-solving, conflict resolution, group dynamics, and change. She can be contacted through her company, Changemakers, at the following address:

Gini Graham Scott, Ph.D.
Director
Changemakers
308 Spruce Street
San Francisco, CA 94118
(415) 567-2747
FAX: (415) 931-8725